Here's What Reade

"The GPS, Loran & Nav/Comm Guide"

"Very good and informative—not just product hype!"
—R.D., Dallas, TX

"Excellent book. Had all the information I was looking for."
—G.S., Lannon, WI

"Has helped me figure out this otherwise confusing subject!"
—J.M., Santa Monica, CA

"Excellent book—only one of its kind."
—D.H., Newton, KS

"Good Stuff. Still reading and referencing it."
—C.S., Miami, FL

"Helpful in making up my mind."
—J.H., Berlin, NH

"Wonderful! I learned a lot!"
—L.N. Lakewood, CO

The GPS, Loran & Nav/Comm Guide

Keith Connes

Butterfield Press

Published by Butterfield Press 990 Winery Canyon Road
Templeton, CA 93465

Sixth edition

Also by Keith Connes: *Know Your Airplane!*

This book is dedicated to my very dear friend Anne Leach, who has not only provided a first-rate index and editing service for every edition, but has also blessed me with a wealth of suggestions that have enhanced the book in so many ways.

ACKNOWLEDGMENTS

The author received generous cooperation from many segments of the aviation industry. Special thanks are due to Murray Smith of *Professional Pilot*, John Stites of Comant Industries, and consulting engineer Walt Dean, for their editorial contributions. For their most helpful input on the Global Positioning System, the author is grateful to George Quinn and Jerry Bradley of the FAA, Cmdr. Dave Olsen of the US Coast Guard, Ralph Eschenbach of Trimble, Ken Bloom of Rockwell, and Doug Carlson of GARMIN.

Bruce Brake was desktop publishing consultant. The book was printed by McNaughton & Gunn, Saline, Michigan, USA.

Photo credits: Product photos were supplied by the manufacturers.

Illustration credits: Fig. 2-1 courtesy of Collins. Figs. 3-1 and 3-2 courtesy of ARNAV. Fig. 3-3 courtesy of Micrologic. Appendix C: GPS antenna illustrations courtesy of Comant; loran antenna illustrations courtesy of ARNAV. Figs. 4-1, 4-2, and 4-3 courtesy of Trimble.

Cover design and illustration on page 14 by Quentin Eckman.

Editing and Index by Anne Leach.

Contents

Foreword 11

Introduction 13

1 **Choosing Your Equipment** 15
How to use this book to select the avionics equipment that best meets your needs.

2 **How the VOR System Works** 17
Three classes of VORs...DME and RNAV: do we still need them?

3 **How the Loran System Works** 21
The master-slave relationship...Watch out for those baseline extensions!

4 **How the GPS System Works** 27
Signals from on high...Degraded by Selective Availability...Super-accurate Differential GPS.

5 **Is Loran Dead?** 33
Several reasons why you might want to use loran, despite the growing popularity of GPS.

6 **GPS & Loran for the IFR Pilot** 35
Overlay and stand-alone approaches...Avoiding the certification nightmare...IFR flight with a VFR set.

7 **How to Shoot a GPS Approach** 41
The automated database...Pushing the right button at the right time...The joy of standardized approaches.

8 **Features to Consider in GPS & Loran Receivers** 45
True cost...Types of display...Ease of use...Databases...SUA alerts...Moving map displays.

9	**Panel-Mounted GPS, Loran & Multi-Sensor Models** Features, specifications, and prices of current models...Hands-On Evaluations.	55
10	**GPS Handhelds** The popular portables...Features, specifications, and prices of current models...Hands-On Evaluations.	91
11	**Various Types of Moving Map Systems** Panel-mounts to laptops... Features, specifications, and prices of current models...Hands-On Evaluations.	108
12	**GPS & Loran Accessories** Fuel Computers... External CDIs...A sophisticated Fuel/Air Data System.	120
13	**Features to Consider in VHF Navs & Comms** Stand-alone or all-in-one?...Sizes and shapes... Frequency storage.	124
14	**Panel-Mounted VHF Navs & Comms** Features, specifications, and prices of current models...Hands-On Evaluations.	127
15	**A New Breed: GPS/Comms** Smart black boxes that help you select the comm frequencies you need, based on your present position.	137
16	**VHF Handhelds** The many uses of VHF handhelds...Criteria for selecting a unit...Features, specifications, and prices.	139
17	**How to Choose a Radio Shop** What is a good installation?...Getting a proper bid... Radios by mail?...Keeping your avionics healthy.	145

Appendices

A **Understanding Latitude & Longitude** **152**
How to determine your lat/lon position using a WAC, sectional, or terminal area chart.

B **A Guide to Guides** **155**
A selection of publications offering useful information to the pilot.

C **GPS & Loran Antenna Installation** **158**
Different types of antennas and their characteristics... Proper placement of GPS and loran antennas.

D **Directory of Manufacturers** **169**
The names, addresses, phone and FAX numbers of the makers of avionics, instruments, and other items.

E **Glossary** **172**
Acronyms, abbreviations, and terms used throughout this book.

Index **179**

Foreword

As pilots, we were all very happy with Loran-C. We could get an accurate groundspeed in any direction—not just going straight to or from a VORTAC. And we knew right where we were. Accuracy was great. Databases were sensational. Of course, we did lose loran every now and then, due to precipitation.

But GPS is with us now, and it really tops loran. It rains the signal down on us anywhere. No holidays—we just don't lose it. GPS will do everything loran does and more, with no precip loss of signal.

There's really no need to wait to buy a GPS unit. Especially if you're armed with the latest book by Keith Connes, his sixth edition of *The GPS, Loran & Nav/Comm Guide.*

Or if your budget is tight, you can pick up one of the still-good loran units, probably used from a radio shop now pushing the newer GPS models. It looks like Loran-C is going to be around for quite some time to come. The talk in key circles of government and the Wild Goose Association (an international forum on loran) has been that we may integrate loran stations with the GPS network, make them sort of ground-based satellites for fixed measurement. So at any rate, the Loran-C stations will still be here so that your loran-based box will continue to work for you for a long time to come.

What unit or units are right for you? Everything you need to know is in the new edition of *The GPS, Loran & Nav/Comm Guide.* I've been a reader of every one of Keith's books, beginning with his first Guide in 1986. Each one has gotten better, provided me with more information. The current sixth edition you have in your hands covers the latest handheld GPS portable units and goes on up through sophisticated systems like the Trimble TNL-3000T I have in my Piper Saratoga.

I have depended on the accurate, thorough, and extremely useful avionics information Keith Connes has written over the past years. And I'm proud to say that Keith will be writing a new series of avionics articles for our magazine, *Pro Pilot,* in the months and years to come.

I find Keith to be a dedicated pilot and a conscientious writer. He flies his own plane, Grumman American Tiger N16LC, has over 8000 hours of flight time, and is a current Commercial Multi/Instrument pilot.

His books are by my bedside. His research has aided me in my own selection of equipment. His sixth edition is his best treatise to date on GPS, loran and VHF equipment as well. I'm sure you'll enjoy the book. More important, I'm sure it will aid you in your own selection of whatever electronic marvels you'll add to your panel.

Happy flying.

Murray Smith, ATP/CFI
Publisher, *Professional Pilot*

Introduction

When I sat down to write the first edition of this book back in 1985, the loran boom was becoming an explosion. New receivers were springing up like daisies, as manufacturers of marine sets began to recognize the importance of the aviation market. (It took awhile for the traditional avionics manufacturers to get the message.)

As time went on, the sets got smarter—many of them acquiring databases that were truly encyclopedic. At the same time, the price spectrum broadened, with plain vanilla receivers trading for as little as a few hundred dollars.

Today, much the same scenario is taking place with the exciting receivers that pull in signals from the Global Positioning System satellites and provide even higher standards of accuracy and reliability.

New GPS models keep bursting on the scene, ranging from relatively low-priced handhelds—some with built-in moving map displays—to panel-mounted units with a mind-boggling array of sophisticated features.

For those who can't decide between GPS and loran, there are the multi-sensor systems that can use *both* types of signals.

Confused as to which is best for you? Relax, you've come to the right book.

This is the sixth edition of a book that has changed titles twice, to keep up with the trend in avionics. The first title was *The Loran, RNAV & Nav/Comm Guide*. This was succeeded by *The Loran, GPS & Nav/Comm Guide*. Now, for a change of emphasis, we have *The GPS, Loran, & Nav/Comm Guide*, with more information than ever on the Global Positioning System and its growing importance as an approved system for aviation navigation. We take a candid look at the pros and cons of both GPS and loran, to help you make an informed decision.

Of course, all the current GPS and loran models are in here, complete with their major features and specifications—and we've added more Hands-On Evaluations, based on personal experience in the air and on the ground.

And let's not forget the VOR system, which is still the basis for the air traffic control system and a must for IFR operations. There have been some interesting developments in the traditional VHF navigation and communications avionics. In addition to such goodies as digital tuning, frequency storage, and built-in ECDIs (electronic course deviation indicators), we have such phenomena as a nav/comm that takes the pulse, so to speak, of your plane's electrical system, another set that *tells* you what frequency you've tuned in, and a couple of others that help you select frequencies based on your current position.

We've got new moving map systems that *show* you where you are—some that fit in the panel, others that fit in your hand, and still others that can send their animated displays to your portable computer.

The wizardry that helps make our flying easier, safer, and more fun seems endless. Well, at least it's enough to fill a book.

I hope you'll enjoy reading and using *The GPS, Loran & Nav/Comm Guide* as much as I've enjoyed putting it together. If you have any questions or comments, I'd like to hear from you. Please write to me in care of Butterfield Press.

Keith Connes

1

Choosing Your Equipment

If you're planning on buying some new avionics for your plane, chances are you're in one of the following situations:

1) You've got a brand new plane with a blank panel—perhaps a homebuilt. Or ...
2) You're modernizing the panel of an older bird by replacing its outmoded radios. Lots of people are going that route these days. It's considerably cheaper than buying a new plane, and let's face it: over the past decade, the aviation industry's most meaningful and affordable design advances have shown up in the black boxes, not the aircraft themselves. Or ...
3) Your present panel is okay, but you're thinking of putting in a box or two that will give you added capability.

Depending on the kind of flying you do, you may find that a GPS or loran receiver—with its ability to tell you where you are, where your destination is, how fast you're traveling, and when you're going to arrive—may serve perfectly well as your primary nav system, and all you'll need to add is a comm radio. (Actually, a couple of manufacturers are now combining GPS receivers and VHF comm transceivers, as an alternative to the traditional VOR-based nav/comms. These are described in the chapter entitled "A New Breed: GPS/Comms.")

On the other hand, VOR receivers are still necessary for many pilots, especially those who fly IFR.

I navigate via GPS or loran (mostly GPS). The steering information is generally more precise and more stable than the signal provided by the VOR receiver, and the wealth of other data that comes out of the GPS or loran receiver's computer greatly simplifies my navigation chores. At the same time, my dual VOR receivers and DME are lighted up as a backup and for conducting IFR approaches.

Your particular preferences may well differ from mine. This book is designed to aid you in the decision-making process by pointing out the relative merits of the VOR, loran, and GPS systems.

If technical writing puts you to sleep, you may be tempted to skip those chapters that explain how each system works. Nevertheless, I urge you to read those chapters—particularly if you plan to enjoy the miracles of GPS or loran navigation. I've tried to keep the writing sufficiently uncomplicated that even I can understand it, and I feel certain that you'll be more comfortable with these computer-intensive systems if you have a grasp of the theory behind them.

Also, become very well acquainted with the operating manual of any set you use. For example, no two GPS or loran manufacturers take the same path in designing their receivers, and virtually each of the models has its own unique combination of features. The differences from model to model are particularly noticeable in the software capabilities and the methods of programming, storing, and retrieving information.

To help clarify the situation, there is a chapter entitled "Features to Consider in GPS & Loran Receivers." Another chapter, "Panel-Mounted GPS, Loran, & Multi-Sensor Models," lists the features and specifications of each individual model. GPS handhelds and the new GPS/Comms are given separate chapters.

Although VHF nav/comm radios sets do not vary from one another as dramatically as GPS and loran receivers, there are significant differences in set design, types of display and frequency management. Again, I describe the advantages of the various features and then go on to list the major features and specs of each model. Handheld transceivers get the same type of analysis in their own chapter.

I have included the manufacturer's suggested list price of each piece of equipment. Although the prices were valid when this book went to press, undoubtedly some of them changed before the ink was dry. More to the point, almost every piece of avionics equipment is discounted at the dealer level. However, the list prices will help you determine the size of the ballpark each model is in.

Now let's get to the meat of the book, starting with a look at the VOR system.

2

How the VOR System Works

VOR is the traditional FAA navigation system. IFR airways, intersections, and other fixes are defined by VOR stations, as are VOR nonprecision approaches. DME and RNAV provide added capabilities. We'll look at each part of the system in turn.

VOR

"VOR" is an acronym for Very high frequency Omnidirectional Range. The VOR system was introduced by the FAA in the '50s, replacing the erratic low frequency "A-N" ranges. It serves as the primary navigation facility for civil aviation in the National Airspace System.

There are approximately 1,000 VOR transmitters operating in the US, on the frequency range of 108.0 to 117.95 MHz. Some are colocated with DME or military TACAN facilities to provide DME information; they are called VOR-DME and VORTAC stations respectively, and for simplicity's sake I'll refer to them as VORTACs where applicable.

Since the VHF band is line-of-sight, reception distance will vary according to the terrain, location of the transmitter, altitude of the airplane, and class of the navaid. There are three classes of VORs. The T (terminal) VOR has a normal usable distance of 25 nm at altitudes of 12,000 feet and below. The L (low altitude) VOR provides a usable signal for 40 nm at altitudes of 18,000 feet and below. The H (high altitude) VOR transmits for 100 nm between 14,500 and 17,999 feet, and 130 nm between 18,000 feet and 45,000 feet.

The VOR station sends out a signal that can be segmented into radials in all 360 degrees of the compass, oriented to magnetic north. Here's how it works: The signal is rotated electrically at 1800 RPM, and there are two navigational signal components. One, called a reference signal, has a constant phase at all points around the transmitter. The two components are in phase at magnetic north and out of phase to a varying degree in all other directions. The VOR receiver measures the phase difference electronically and presents this in the form of radial information.

Left-right steering information is shown on your CDI or HSI in terms of angular deviation, with a full-scale needle deflection representing a deviation of 10 degrees (in the nav mode). How this translates into the *distance* you are off course depends on how far you are from the station.

For example, as you will see in Fig. 2-1 (left), a full-scale (10-degree) needle deflection indicates that you are 5.3 nm off course when you are 30 nm from the station, whereas the course error becomes 17.6 nm when you are 100 nm from the station. (At the risk of stating the obvious, I must add that if the needle is *pegged* at the end of the scale, you could be even *further* off course.)

While VOR is usually quite accurate when ground and airborne equipment are operating within tolerances, there are anomalies, such as course bends and "scalloping" in some geographical areas, as well as the inevitable "cone of confusion" close to the station.

Unlike the GPS and loran receivers, which utilize three or more stations to establish the aircraft's position, the VOR receiver tunes in only one station at a time and indicates the plane's position relative to

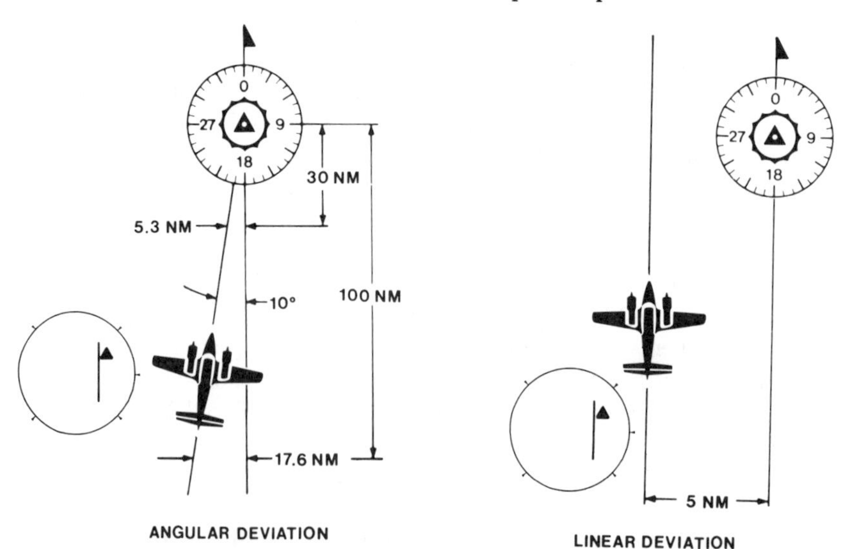

Fig. 2-1 (Left) VOR equipment provides angular deviation. The off-course distance represented by a given amount of CDI needle deflection decreases as you approach the station. (Right) By contrast, the linear deviation provide by RNAV and loran equipment remains constant.

a radial, or track, emanating from that station. To fix the aircraft's position along that track, the pilot must either tune in a second VOR station or utilize other equipment, such as DME or ADF.

In addition to its navigation capabilities, a VOR station can serve as a voice communication link with an associated Flight Service Station, and some facilities also provide TWEB (transcribed weather broadcast) service.

DME

In my view, DME (distance measuring equipment) is practically obsolete, considering that even the least expensive loran or GPS receiver is far better at performing the same functions. RNAV equipment, which utilizes DME and VOR, is likewise outmoded. The only reason for continuing to give panel space (and space in this book) to these boxes is that there are still some instrument approaches that involve the use of DME and RNAV.

DME works in partnership with your VOR to give you distance and groundspeed information. The onboard DME equipment transmits paired pulses. A VORTAC station responds by sending its own paired pulses back to the aircraft's DME equipment, which measures the time interval between the interrogating and reply pulses, and translates this into the distance between the plane and the station.

This computation is called slant range distance because it is the distance from the plane at altitude, slanting down to the station at ground level. Thus, if the plane passes over a VORTAC at 5,000 feet, its DME will show that the VORTAC is still a mile away, which indeed it is—straight down.

The DME set is able to compute and display groundspeed based on the rate at which the distance to the VORTAC changes. For an accurate groundspeed readout, the plane must be navigating directly to or from the VORTAC. In addition, as the plane gets close to the station, slant range error theoretically would cause a gross distortion of the groundspeed readout. However, a modern DME can detect this situation and will hold in display the last known accurate groundspeed during station passage.

Since it knows the distance to the VORTAC and the aircraft's groundspeed, the DME can also compute your ETE (estimated time enroute, sometimes referred to as time-to-station)—or, if it is equipped with a real-time clock—your ETA (estimated time of arrival).

The DME is channeled, or tuned, through one of the aircraft's VOR receivers. Many DMEs have a HOLD function that enables you to continue receiving DME information while tuning the VOR set to another frequency. For example, you can place the VORTAC you are using on HOLD, then tune in a localizer frequency for an approach. The DME will continue to display groundspeed, distance and time-to-station to the previously tuned VORTAC, while your CDI or HSI shows course deviation information for the localizer you have subsequently tuned in.

RNAV

The acronym RNAV stands for "area navigation," and although there are various kinds of area navigation systems, RNAV is generally applied to the VORTAC-based system.

The heart of an RNAV set is its computer, which works with an onboard VOR receiver and a DME, one or both of which are sometimes packaged with the RNAV set to form an integrated unit. The major function of the RNAV equipment is to electronically "move" a VORTAC from its actual location to a user-selected location called a phantom waypoint. For example, suppose you want to fly direct to Hometown Airport, but there is no navaid at the field. However, Nearby VORTAC is located 25 nm southeast of Hometown. With your RNAV set, you can use Nearby to set up a waypoint, or phantom VORTAC, at Hometown.

You do this by programming Nearby VORTAC's frequency into the RNAV's computer, along with the radial (315 degrees) and distance (25 nm) from the VORTAC to the desired waypoint. Thus you have virtually created a VORTAC at Hometown.

Again, all of this and more can be accomplished with greater ease and finesse by means of a GPS or loran receiver. True, there are some published RNAV nonprecision approaches, but nobody will want to conduct them once they are duplicated by GPS approaches. (This will be equally true of VOR approaches and—except for those afflicted with serious masochistic tendencies—NDB approaches.)

Add to this the fact that Bendix/King's KNS 81—the only general aviation RNAV system that is likely to be in production by the end of 1994—lists for $7,449 and up, DME not included—and you can readily see why the future of RNAV is not very bright.

Be that as it may, the acronym continues to have star billing in the traffic controllers' lexicon; when you file an IFR flight plan and want a straight-arrow routing to your destination, regardless of the equipment on board, you ask for "RNAV-direct."

Now let's take a look at the loran system.

3

How the Loran System Works

Using its sophisticated computer brain, a loran set can give you the bearing and distance from your present position to any place on earth. In addition, once you are airborne, even the simplest of loran sets will display your groundspeed and ETE (estimated time enroute), and will provide left-right steering corrections to keep you on course. The more sophisticated models will give you a lot more information; for details, see the chapters entitled "Features to Consider in a GPS or Loran GPS Receiver" and "Panel-Mounted GPS, Loran, & Multi-Sensor Models."

Now that GPS has become so popular, is loran worth considering? The answer is "yes, if you like to save money." Loran sets can be purchased for less than half the price of a comparable GPS model; this is explored further in the chapter entitled "Is Loran Dead?"

If you're accustomed to navigating via the VOR system, you'll find that loran is quite a different breed of cat. But with all its blessings, the loran system is burdened with some shortcomings that, under certain circumstances, could provide you with unreliable information. Therefore, to use loran effectively and safely, you should understand how the system works, what to look for, and why. So here comes the technical stuff. Follow me through.

The Loran Chains

At this writing, there are 21 loran chains worldwide, of which 12 serve the US and Canada. Each chain is made up of a master station, designated M, and from two to five secondary stations, designated V, W, X, Y, and Z.

These stations broadcast at 100 KHz, which is in the low frequency band. Low frequency signals follow the curvature of the earth and can be picked up from much greater distances than the VHF line-of-sight signals used in the VOR system. This is why a relatively small number of loran stations can provide broad coverage.

Your loran receiver gets its position information from the particular chain or chains that provide optimum coverage for the area in which you are flying. (Some loran sets receive only one chain at a time while others have multi-chain capability.) Starting with the master, each station sends out a group of pulsed signals. The master station transmits nine pulses, with a pause between the eighth and ninth pulses. Then each secondary in turn sends out a group of eight pulses. There is an emission delay of different length between the pulse groups transmitted by each station. The master is further distinguished from its secondaries by phase coding, in which certain pulses within a group are inverted.

Each Chain Has its Own GRI

So far, we have discussed the ways in which the various stations within a chain are identified. Now let's see how the chain itself is distinguished from other chains. The time that elapses from the beginning of one master pulse group to the beginning of the next—called the GRI (group repetition interval)—is different for each chain. The GRI is measured in microseconds (millionths of a second) and that measurement, with the last zero omitted, is used to identify the chain. For example, the Great Lakes chain has a GRI of 89,700 microseconds and is referred to as GRI 8970.

A typical loran receiver contains an oscillator that works rather like a very sophisticated stopwatch, measuring the time difference (TD) between the arrival of the master signal and the arrival of the signals from each of the available secondaries. All points that represent the same TD between the master and a given secondary would form a hyperbolic, i.e., symmetrically curved, line of position (LOP) if drawn on a chart. An LOP, then, is actually a line of constant time difference. Your loran receiver, with its built-in computer, can establish that it is somewhere on a particular LOP between the master and that secondary.

But exactly where? To get the answer, the set needs a second TD, derived from the master and another secondary. This provides another LOP that will intersect the first LOP, and the aircraft's position is thus established at the intersection of the two LOPs.

(In reality, two LOPs, if extended far enough, will intersect each other at *two* places, but unless the curvature is extreme, those two places will be sufficiently far apart that the loran's computer can determine which intersection represents the aircraft's position.)

The computer then translates this fix into the latitude and longitude coordinates of the aircraft's present position. This is done by means of an earth model that has the lat/lon coordinates of the loran transmitters in the computer's memory. Latitude and longitude serve as the position reference of loran (and GPS), just as radial and distance serve as the position reference of the VOR system. (Some loran and GPS sets can convert latitude and longitude to radial and distance from a waypoint, and vice versa, for the convenience of the user.)

As the plane moves from one position to another, the computer establishes its direction of flight and groundspeed. If a route of flight has been entered, in the form of two or more waypoints, the set can also display such navigation information as bearing and distance to the destination waypoint, crosstrack error, and ETE or ETA.

A number of factors are necessary for accurate navigation. The computer needs to know the rate at which the signal has traveled to the receiver from each transmitter. That rate—roughly six microseconds for one nautical mile—is relatively constant over sea water, but is slower over land, and varies according to the shape and conductivity of the ground.

This anomaly is known as *additional secondary phase factor* (ASF), and loran manufacturers compensate for it in different ways. A common method is to take loran readings at numerous locations at which the exact lat/lon coordinates are known, and then introduce a lat/lon correction table into the software. (Some models also permit the user to enter small ASF corrections.)

The Importance of Good Geometry

It is necessary to have good signal geometry in order to get an accurate fix, and this requires the proper choice of GRI, followed by the selection of the best stations to use within that chain. Some units will choose or recommend the proper GRI, while others require you to make that determination. Most modern lorans automatically select the best secondaries.

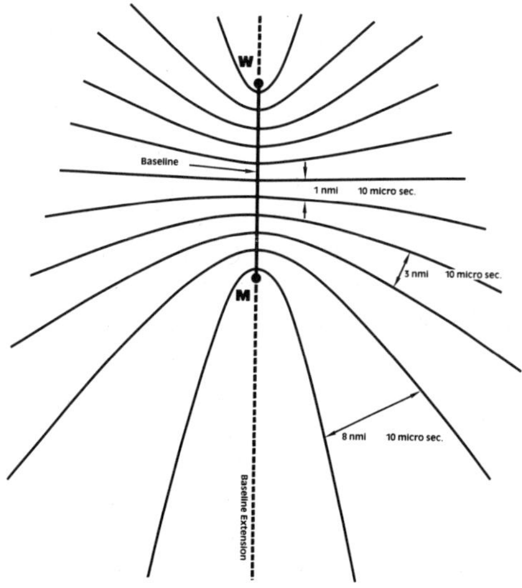

Fig. 3-1. The distance represented by a unit of time distance increases as the lines of position diverge from each other

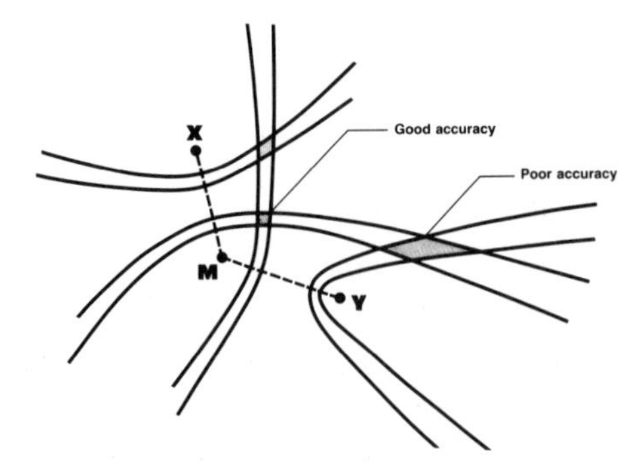

Fig. 3-2 The area of ambiguity near Station Y is greatest because of the acute crossing angles.

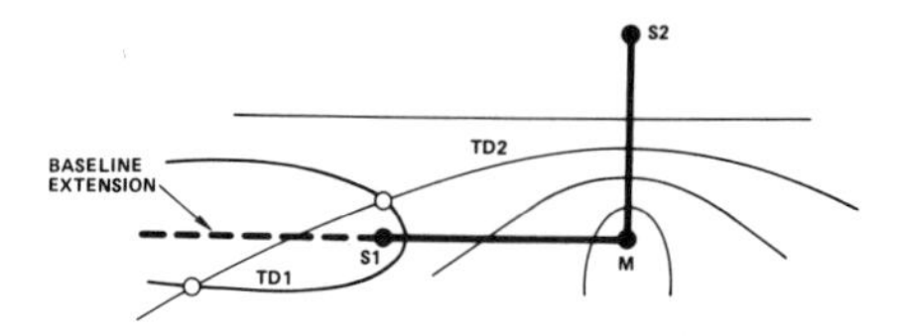

Fig. 3-3. The extreme curvature of an LOP at a baseline extension could result in two possible positions (indicated by circles) that are close to each other. The loran set could choose the wrong one, producing a large error.

Getting good geometry is complicated by the fact that the curvature of the LOPs is greatest near the transmitter sites. Therefore, the distance represented by a unit of time difference will increase as the LOPs spread away from each other. For example, if you will look at Fig. 3-1, you will see that the difference of 10 microseconds between two LOPs near the center of the baseline (an imaginary line drawn between a master and a secondary) might represent 1 nm, whereas that same TD of 10 microseconds at the baseline extension could mean a distance of 8 nm or more.

The ideal crossing angle of two LOPs is 90 degrees. Fig. 3-2 shows how the area of ambiguity increases as the crossing angles become more acute—and again, this is at its worst at the baseline extension.

There's yet another problem endemic to the baseline extension. As I indicated earlier, two LOPs actually form two intersections, but in most cases the intersections are far apart and the correct one can easily be selected by the computer. However, because of the extreme curvature of the LOP in the baseline extension, the two intersections could be close enough to cause the computer to make the wrong choice. (See Fig. 3-3.)

The moral of all of this is, watch for inaccuracies when flying near a baseline extension.

Diagnostics

Your loran receiver will provide you with a variety of diagnostics to help you to determine the validity of the nav information it's putting out. These diagnostics are usually displayed in a non-navigation mode, generally called "setup" or "aux."

Also, a warning message may appear regardless of the mode you're using, if the nav information is below a certain standard. This warning will appear when you first fire up the set, since it normally takes two or three minutes for the receiver to acquire a triad (usually the master and two secondaries). Here are some of the criteria to be aware of:

Signal-to-noise ratio (SNR) is the relationship of the loran signal to unwanted interference. This noise could come from thunderstorm activity, power lines, telephone relay equipment, etc. The loran set's diagnostic mode will probably display a numerical value for the SNR of each of the stations in use. Unfortunately, the numerical values are determined arbitrarily by the loran manufacturers, so there is no consistency from one make to another.

Envelope-to-cycle discrepancy (ECD) is an indication that the loran receiver has focused on the wrong part of the broadcast pulse envelope. As we discussed earlier, the loran receiver establishes its position by measuring the TDs, and in order to do this precisely it must time one point on a given cycle. That point is located by examining the shape, or envelope, of the pulse. If the envelope becomes distorted, there can be a change in the ECD, which, if large enough, can result in a cycle slip.

Blink is the term that describes a special code that a loran transmitter sends out to indicate an abnormality in its transmission. If the station's operating parameters are out of tolerance, the first two pulses of the group being transmitted will blink off and on. The loran set will display some kind of warning message when it receives the blink code. There may also be a warning message if the aircraft is in such a location that the set is getting poor geometry, or some failure is taking place in the unit itself.

If all this sounds complicated, remember that while loran works very well most of the time, things can go wrong under a variety of conditions. So it behooves you to become very familiar with the operation of your loran set, read the owner's manual carefully and review it from time to time—and don't rely exclusively on loran for your nav information.

The next chapter describes the Global Positioning System.

4

How the GPS System Works

Now that so many of us have been enjoying the benefits of loran navigation, here comes a system that uses signals from satellites to provide position information that's even more precise than loran, and more complete to boot.

The system is called GPS, which stands for the Global Positioning System. It is operated by the Department of Defense for military purposes, but civilian users are able to benefit from it as well. Is GPS for you? Has it made loran obsolete? How does it work, anyhow? In this chapter, we'll deal with these and other questions about the Global Positioning System.

Let's begin by looking at how GPS works.

Like loran, GPS establishes the position of a receiver-equipped aircraft—or boat, or car, or even an individual carrying a portable unit—by means of intersecting LOPs (lines of position).

As we discussed in the chapter entitled "How Loran Works," the loran system creates LOPs by comparing the time differences of the transmissions of three or more stations. The transmitters are, of course, planted firmly on the ground and their positions are stored in the receiver's computer.

By contrast, the GPS transmissions come from satellites that are moving rapidly in orbit nearly 11,000 miles above the earth. This makes things a little trickier; nevertheless, the GPS receiver has an almanac database that tells it where each satellite is scheduled to be at any given time.

A typical satellite weighs in at 1739 pounds, which is just a bit more than a grossed-out Cessna 152. Each satellite transmits on the L-band frequencies of 1575.42 MHz (L1) and 1227.6 MHz (L2). Like VOR/DME, and unlike loran, the satellite frequency spectrum is line-of-sight. Therefore, a satellite must be in view of the aircraft receiver's antenna in order to be used for navigation.

LOPs in 3-D

If you had a perfect clock, your GPS receiver would need the services of three satellites to determine your position. Let's start with one satellite, and say that your receiver calculates (by a method I'll describe shortly) that this particular satellite is 11,000 miles from you. Well, if you were to tie an 11,000-mile-long string to the satellite and pull it in every possible direction, the free end of the string would describe an imaginary sphere having a radius of

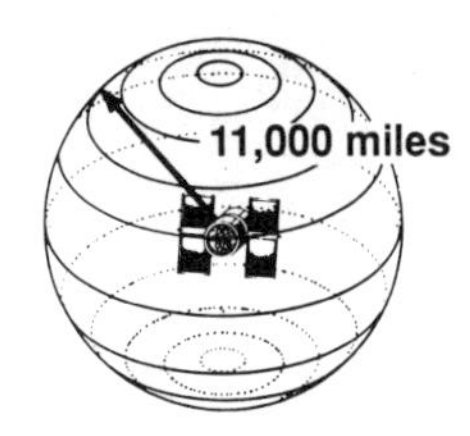

Fig. 4-1. You are somewhere on this sphere

11,000 miles. You are somewhere on that sphere (Fig. 4-1).

That covers a lot of territory, but you can narrow it down considerably by determining your distance from a second satellite whose position is also known. If you find that you are 12,000 miles from that satellite, you have created a second imaginary sphere, and your location must fall somewhere on a circle formed by the intersection of the two spheres (Fig. 4-2). A third sphere from a third satellite will intersect the circle at two points, and you are at one of those points (Fig. 4-3). Which one? That's easily determined, because only one point will make sense, and your receiver's computer can figure out which one that is.

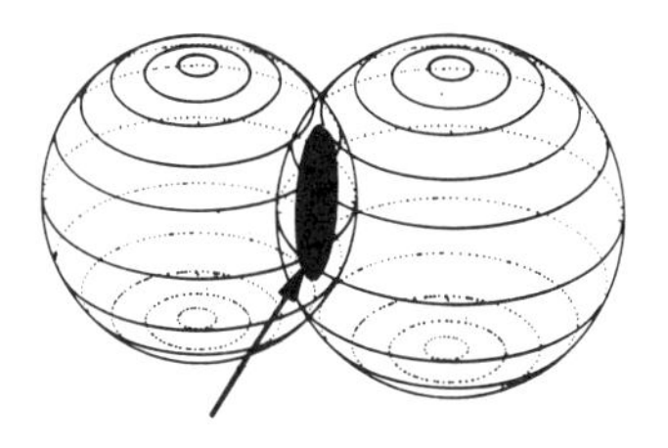

Fig. 4-2. Two measurements put you somewhere on this circle.

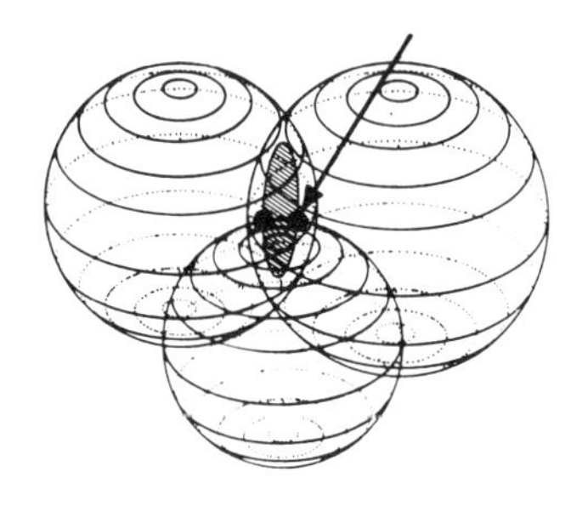

Fig. 4-3. Three measurements put you at one of two points.

But remember, to create those three spheres, you had to know your distance from each satellite you were using, and this is calculated by a simple mathematical formula you've used often in the cockpit: time x speed = distance. If you've flown for two hours at a groundspeed of 120 knots, you've covered a distance of 240 nautical miles, right?

In the same way, your distance from a given satellite is arrived at by establishing the length of time it takes a signal from the satellite to reach the receiver, and multiplying that time span by the speed of the signal—which is the speed of light, or 186,000 miles per second.

How does your receiver know when the signal leaves the satellite? The signal is sent in the form of a digital code—actually called a pseudo-random code because the pulses seem to be sent out in random fashion, but really are not. The receiver is generating the identical code, shifting it until it locks onto the transmitted code. When that occurs, the information the receiver acquires tells it when the code was transmitted. This enables the receiver to compute the time difference—the amount of time it took for the satellite's signal to travel to the receiver—and thus compute the range.

Synchronize Your Watches, Gentlemen

For an accurate computation, the satellites and the GPS receiver must be marching in time with each other, and that's an understatement! Consider that if the receiver's clock disagrees with a satellite's time signal by one thousandth of a second, the resulting position fix could be off by 186 miles, which is, shall we say, an unacceptable error.

There are four atomic clocks on board each satellite, and their timekeeping ability is measured in nanoseconds. (A nanosecond is one-billionth of a second.) Their accuracy is not absolute; these clocks are expected to lose one second in about 70,000 years. They darn well should keep good time, since they go for about $100,000 apiece, and the economic facts of life demand that our receivers have to make do with clocks that are good but not that good. So from a scientific point of view, the receiver doesn't really know what time it is. Thus there are four unknowns that must be solved: latitude, longitude, altitude, and time.

There's a mathematical truism that tells us that in order to solve for four unknowns, we must have four equations. Therefore, we need to have four satellites in view in order to establish an accurate position.

We also need to correct for each satellite's actual position, ionospheric and atmospheric conditions, and a time difference caused by the very motion of the satellites. (As Einstein explained in his theory of relativity, a clock in a fast-moving vehicle, if it could be seen by a stationary observer, would appear to go slower than a stationary timepiece. So if there were no compensation for the satellite's motion, we would see a 38-microsecond drift of time in a 24-hour period, which would result in a position error of about six nautical miles.)

The satellites transmit the necessary corrective data, called ephemeris, to a ground-based network consisting of a control station at Falcon Air Force Base in Colorado and remote sites at Cape Canaveral, Ascencion, Diego Garcia, and Kwajalein. Updates of the navigation messages are sent back to the satellites several times a day.

Now that we've seen how GPS works, let's see if it makes sense for you to start taking advantage of it.

It's Official: GPS is Up and Running

The Global Positioning System has been designed to utilize a constellation of 24 satellites, criss-crossing the sky in orbits of 11 hours and 58 minutes in duration. At this writing, 26 satellites are up there and more will be launched, replacing the older vehicles that, like old soldiers, are fading away. The DoD has declared the system IOC (initial operational capability), which means that most of the time, and in most places, you should be able to receive at least the four satellites necessary to provide latitude, longitude, altitude, and time for 3-D navigation.

2-D from Three Satellites

At certain times and in certain locations, you may not have four satellites in view. If you can receive three satellites (and three is the barebones minimum for GPS navigation), your receiver can derive the two dimensions of latitude and longitude, plus time. However, since GPS is a three-dimensional system, your receiver will have to be given altitude input either by manual pilot entry or from another source, such as an encoding altimeter. This input will not be precise, and that in turn will affect the accuracy of the lat/lon solution, but computations made under these conditions will be adequate for VFR navigation.

Incidentally, you will notice that when you are receiving four or more satellites, your GPS-generated altitude readout will probably differ from the altitude indicated by your altimeter—and the higher you are, the greater that difference is likely to be. That's due to a combination of errors inherent in a conventional barometric altimeter.

Degraded Accuracy for Us Ordinary Civilians

There are two types of GPS navigation service: the Precise Positioning Service (PPS) and the Standard Positioning Service (SPS).

SPS is provided on the L1 frequency, which contains a coarse acquisition (C/A) code and a navigation data message. The L1 and L2 frequencies also contains a precision (P) code that is part of the PPS, but is not included in the SPS.

The PPS is designed to achieve a position accuracy of at least 17.8 meters (58.4 feet) horizontally and 27.7 meters (90.9 feet) vertically. Sounds pretty good, doesn't it? The only problem is, we ordinary civilians will have to find other ways to achieve this type of accuracy, as the Precise Positioning Service is reserved for the military and certain other authorized users.

We "plane folks" and other common taxpayers get to use the Standard Positioning Service, which in its normal state can be almost as accurate as the PPS. However, for security reasons, the DoD at its discretion deliberately degrades the SPS to provide an accuracy, based on approximately 95 percent probability, of about 100 meters (328 feet) horizontally and 156 meters (512 feet) vertically. This degradation is euphemistically called Selective Availability. (Ironically, Selective Availability had to be turned off during Desert Storm because only civilian GPS units were obtainable in the quantities immediately needed by our armed forces.)

And, as I indicated earlier, these accuracy figures are contingent on the operation of the complete satellite constellation.

More Accurate Approaches with DGPS

There's another acronym to add to our thick bowl of alphabet soup. DGPS is Differential GPS, an enhancement to the system consisting of ground-based datalink stations that measure errors in the satellite signals, using their known position as a reference, and broadcast correction figures to aircraft in the vicinity. If one of these stations is located adjacent to an airport runway, an aircraft's GPS receiver can utilize this information to overcome Selective Availability. A plan is under consideration to provide nationwide coverage with 30 or 40 of these ground-based stations, linked to about three INMARSAT III geostationary satellites.

So What About Loran?

With so much attention being lavished on satellite navigation, where does this leave loran? Loran receivers are still being marketed. Should you consider buying one? We'll deal with that subject in the next chapter.

5

Is Loran Dead?

No question about it, GPS has overtaken loran in the minds of the FAA, aircraft manufacturers, and consumers—for the following reasons:

GPS provides worldwide coverage; loran does not, and probably never will.

GPS has the potential of far greater position accuracy than loran.

Whereas loran reception can be disrupted by rain, snow, or a nearby thunderstorm, GPS signals are not affected by these weather phenomena.

This is not to say that GPS is flawless; in addition to the DoD's deliberate degradation by Selective Availability, GPS accuracy and reliability can be affected by such factors as satellite geometry, atomic clock inaccuracies, atmospheric propagation delays, signal reflections, receiver processing errors, and errors in satellite ephemeris data. However, these anomalies are, for the most part, relatively small.

GPS has moved ahead of loran in terms of IFR certification. While some loran receivers are certifiable for enroute and terminal operations, no manufacturer appears to be interested anymore in gaining approval for nonprecision approaches. By contrast, more and more GPS models will become certifiable for enroute, terminal, and nonprecision approach operations—and, in time, for precision approaches as well. (For further information, see the chapter entitled "GPS & Loran for the IFR Pilot.")

Does this mean that loran is dead? No, but stand-alone loran models are decreasing in number. II Morrow has discontinued production of their Flybuddy loran and Bendix/King no longer makes the KLN 88. (Northstar and ARNAV are still offering stand-alone lorans—at least for the time being.)

Because of the market emphasis on GPS, the pilot on a tight budget can have a good choice of loran trade-ins at very attractive prices. However, bear in mind that new loran sets will be produced only as long as there is a sufficient demand for them. Eventually, all stand-alone loran receivers are likely to be discontinued, and when that happens, it is questionable whether such support as database updates will continue to be available. On the other hand, production of multi-sensor systems, utilizing both loran and GPS signals, will probably go on for a longer period of time, for those who want the security of redundancy.

Loran as a navigation system will continue to exist for the foreseeable future. Some European and Asian countries have indicated that they will be building new loran stations. And in the US, loran could be a method of providing the equivalent of RAIM (receiver autonomous integrity monitoring) that GPS receivers must incorporate in order to be certified for IFR approaches.

Despite loran's ongoing potential, the Coast Guard—which maintains the system in the US—is currently sending out feelers about decommissioning the loran stations in the year 2000 or possibly earlier. Industry and user groups are up in arms, and the outcome remains to be seen.

In sum, loran is not dead, but its future is in some question. This is unfortunate, because the system provides very good navigational capabilities most of the time, throughout the US and in many other parts of the world.

If you presently own a loran receiver and its performance and features meet your needs, you needn't be in a hurry to sacrifice it simply because GPS is the hot new system. In the future, GPS receivers will come down in price and they'll undoubtedly have even more exciting features than we've seen so far. If you're the patient, disciplined type (I, for one, am not), it may suit you to wait awhile.

6

GPS & Loran for the IFR Pilot

When you buy a VOR receiver, you take it for granted that the set (if properly calibrated) can be used for all IFR operations—enroute, terminal and approach. That's because VOR has been the basic foundation of the FAA navigation system since its inception.

This is not true of either GPS or loran navigation. For a little historical perspective, let's start with loran.

Loran was developed primarily for use on ships and boats, and most of the loran stations are operated by the US Coast Guard. In truth, the FAA was forced to accept the reality of loran as a legitimate form of aircraft navigation by the fact that pilots were putting loran receivers into their planes and using them to get from one place to another.

Enter the TSOs

To its credit, the FAA responded positively and developed TSO C60b, which established criteria for certification of loran receivers for IFR enroute and terminal procedures. As a result, a number of models are certifiable for those procedures. A program to implement nonprecision loran approaches was also developed and, in fact, ten approaches were actually issued and published. However, efforts on the part of manufacturers to get their sets approved for approaches evaporated when the GPS boom materialized.

Initially, all GPS receivers were strictly VFR, as loran sets were at first. Then the multi-sensor TSO C115a was created for systems that have both loran and GPS sensors. In essence, the TSO says that you can use the GPS portion of the system for IFR enroute and terminal operations provided that its position information agrees, within certain tolerances, with the loran sensor's position information. In other words, if the GPS sensor is not certified, then it must operate under the supervision of the certified loran sensor.

TSOs with Class

And now GPS has its own TSO, namely C129, which is subdivided into a number of classes. Most of the general aviation equipment will be certifiable under Classes A1 and A2.

GPS receivers that meet Class A1 specs are certifiable for GPS enroute, terminal, and nonprecision approach operations. GPS receivers that meet Class A2 specs are certifiable for enroute and terminal operations, but not approaches.

Classes B1 and B2 provide the same types of approvals, but refer to integrated navigation systems, such as flight management and multi-sensor systems—although the latter can apparently be certified under A1 as well.

Overlay and Stand-alone Approaches

The GPS approaches that are available at this writing are actually overlay approaches. That means they are, in effect, superimposed on underlying ground-based nonprecision approaches, such as VOR, VOR-DME, RNAV, NDB and NDB-DME approaches—and they are flown using the same procedures as those approaches. (Localizer, LDA, and SDF approaches do not qualify as underlying approaches.) However, automatic sequencing from one waypoint to the next, along with other computer-generated aids, makes GPS approaches a lot easier and smoother than their traditional counterparts. (For more on this, see the chapter entitled "How to Shoot a GPS Approach.")

Overlay approaches are very nice to have, but the next phase will give us what we want most of all: stand-alone GPS approaches at airports that don't have any other approaches. The FAA is currently estimating 300 to 400 of them by the end of 1994, with new ones added thereafter at the rate of 400 to 600 per year.

Precision Approaches

Thus far, we have been discussing nonprecision approaches, for which there is no vertical guidance. But GPS, you'll recall, is a 3-D system that determines your plane's altitude as well as its lat/lon position; this opens the door to precision approaches with GPS-derived vertical guidance. (However, DO NOT use GPS-derived altitude for approaches or any other type of altitude information; it will not agree with your barometric altimeter and could seriously compromise your safety.) A supplemental system, utilizing ground-based stations, geostationary satellites, or some other methodology, will be required to compensate for the DoD's Selective Availability that periodically degrades the accuracy of civilian GPS.

According to current estimates, we can expect to start shooting GPS precision approaches in the early part of 1997. Yet another TSO will be generated for this purpose.

It'll Cost You

As these words are being written, some GPS receivers are strictly VFR, and that includes all of the handhelds. Others are certifiable for enroute and terminal, but not for approaches; that's because they were designed and manufactured before the approach criteria emanated from the FAA. Those sets will have to go back to the factory for an upgrade for approach capability, probably to the tune of around a thousand dollars. (GARMIN leap-frogged from the strictly VFR 150 to the A1-certifiable 155; some other manufacturers are taking the same route.)

What Does "IFR-Certified" Really Mean?

You may have noticed that I favor the term *certifiable* as opposed to *certified.* Is there a significant difference? You bet there is!

IFR certification is issued on a plane-by-plane basis. Thus, the "IFR certified" model you buy off the shelf has been approved, through the STC process, for the *factory's* airplane. For any other airplane, the set is IFR *certifiable,* meaning it can, in theory, be certified for your bird. But the ball is in your court. If you want it certified, *you* get it certified.

You can accomplish this by either an STC or a Form 337, depending on the level of your tolerance for pain. Actually, the 337 is the way to go, and since the groundwork has been laid by the factory's TSO and STC, this should be no big deal. In theory.

The problem is, you have to get the paperwork signed off by the avionics inspector of a FSDO. As you probably know, FSDOs are independent fiefdoms scattered all over the country. They are somewhat connected with their parent monarchy, the FAA in Washington, in most respects—the major exception being standardization. I am convinced that the honchos at McDonald's headquarters exercise more control over their hamburger franchises than the administrators at 800 Independence Avenue exert over "their" FSDOs.

Certification: Routine or Nightmare?

So your expenditures of time and money, and your intake in anguish, will depend on the personality and other character traits of the avionics inspector you encounter. To put it another way, the journey you take through this procedure can be either fairly routine or it can turn into a series of tribulations that make the voyage of Odysseus look like a weekend on the Love Boat.

I'll give you a highly abbreviated version of an experience I had getting a set certified for IFR. In this case, it was a KLN 88 loran that was in my plane at the time. My first step was to have the shop that installed the set arrange for the certification. Unfortunately, that shop is ruled by an avionics inspector for whom the term *CYA* has an almost religious significance. Now, are you ready for this? The avionics inspector informed my shop that the airplane flight manual supplement, required as part of the certification process, had to be prepared by a DER (designated engineering representative), who, it turned out, expected a fee of $3,000 for his exertions. On hearing this, I decided to shop around.

After considerable reaching out, I learned that the avionics department of an FBO called Cinema Air was quite expert at getting certification via the San Diego FSDO inspector, an FAA staffer who was in touch with reality. No DER needed. I seized the opportunity and flew to Cinema Air's facility at McClellan-Palomar Airport in Carlsbad, California.

Receiver and Eyeballs Must Agree

Jerry Henry, the shop manager, went over my installation with the proverbial fine tooth comb, and then we went flying. Before takeoff, we inserted a "present position" waypoint at the departure end of Runway 24. Then we conducted a round robin flight over Oceanside VOR, Julian VOR, and Escondido NDB, terminating with our landing on Runway 24. The objective was to verify that the set's computer and our eyeballs were in agreement as we passed over these waypoints. They were.

I received my Form 337 in less than two weeks. Oh, yes, the flight manual supplement: It turned out to be a nine-page document that was virtually a word-for-word copy of the one provided by Bendix/King, except for the insertion of my plane's type, registration and serial number. For this I needed to spend $3,000 on a DER?

Jerry tells me the procedures are pretty much the same for GPS certification as they are for loran. One difference: many VHF comm transmitters are interfering with GPS reception on certain frequencies; his solution is to install an RF (radio frequency) trap.

If you decide to go the certification route, this is my advice: Try to locate a FSDO whose avionics inspector has some understanding of the real world. Then work with a shop in that territory that has a successful history of getting the necessary rubber stamp and signature on a Form 337 for the unit of your choice, at a cost in money and time that is acceptable to you. I can't promise that this will be easy.

After the Agony, the Ecstasy

I've expended a lot of words detailing the possible (though not necessarily inevitable) pain of getting your GPS or loran receiver IFR certified. Now let's look at the rewards.

With an IFR-certified set, you can file "RNAV direct." That term applies to a direct routing, bypassing the airways dog-legs, by an approved means of area navigation equipment. Whether or not ATC grants your request depends largely on when and where you're going from and to. To help your wish come true, it's generally best to request a routing to a navaid, then RNAV direct to a gate or other ATC-favored waypoint that's near your destination.

Even if ATC turns thumbs down and issues the usual clearance via airways, at some point during your flight you can ask Center if you can please now proceed direct to the desired waypoint. If you've included in your flight plan the appropriate suffix indicating that you have the approved equipment (/C, /R, or /W), the controller may give you a green light. Often you won't even have to ask. On many of my flights, a controller has come out of the blue with a "proceed direct," providing a welcome shortcut that has saved time and operating costs.

Important: When you're going direct, be sure you've requested and received a high enough altitude to clear obstructions. Remember, you won't have a published MEA when you're off airways, so check your path of flight against a WAC, sectional, or Jepp RNAV chart. An additional aid is the minimum safe altitude feature that's resident in some receivers. In any case, don't depend on the controller for obstruction clearance; *you're* flying the plane.

Other GPS and loran benefits are very useful during IFR operations, especially the DME-like functions that work even when you're not navigating from or to a VORTAC. For example, the groundspeed readout can help you determine your winds in holding patterns and on approaches. If your set has a database that includes intersections, navigating to an intersection becomes a positive pleasure; you'll get bearing, distance, and ETE without the knob-twisting and arithmetic required by dual VORs.

Are You Better Off with a VFR Set?

What separates an IFR-certifiable receiver from its VFR counterparts? A lot of testing and documentation to show that the unit and its software have met the exacting criteria established by the FAA for IFR operations. A VFR unit may have been built to meet the same standards, or higher, but the manufacturer has not chosen to prove it to the FAA via the costly certification process. In some cases, the manufacturer has elected to remain VFR for the same kind of reason that you may sometimes prefer to fly VFR even though you are instrument rated: *freedom of movement*. There are continuous advances in microprocessor and software development, but the IFR certification process tends to inhibit change.

IFR Flight with a VFR Set

Suppose the model you have chosen is not IFR certified; can you use it during the enroute and terminal portions of an IFR flight? Perhaps, in a limited way. Let's start with the negatives. You may not use it as the basis for specifying an RNAV equipment suffix (/C, /R, or /W) in a flight plan or requesting "RNAV direct," nor may you use a VFR set as your primary source of navigation while IFR.

What you might want to do is evaluate the information provided by your VFR GPS or loran, while navigating with your VOR receiver. For example, if your GPS or loran receiver is right on the money each time you pass over a VOR station or other checkpoint, you can probably put a high degree of faith in the groundspeed and ETE information it's handing out. The main thing is, keep a running check on the set's accuracy and do not use it as your primary source of navigation.

Yes or No?

Should you or shouldn't you buy an IFR set? It's certainly going to cost more money than a comparable VFR model, but if you fly in actual IMC (instrument meteorological conditions), you really should consider the IFR version—especially one that can be certified for those GPS approaches that are becoming available. However, you might want to wait until there's a good selection of Class A1 models out there; as always, competition tends to drive prices down.

7

How to Shoot a GPS Approach

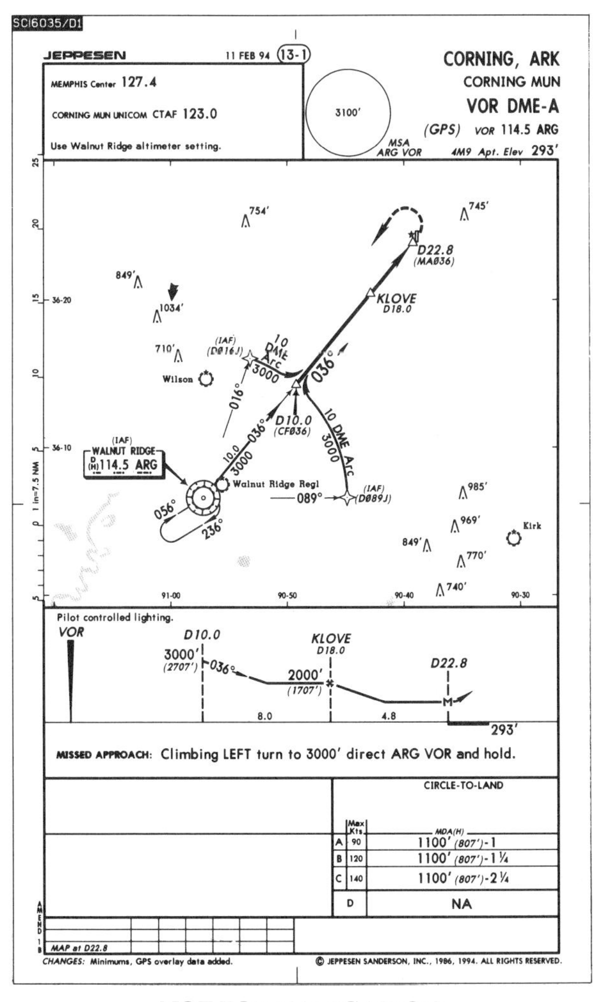

NOT FOR NAVIGATION

What's it like to shoot a GPS approach? Well, it's not like any other type of approach you may have executed. I was given the opportunity to get my feet wet, shortly after GARMIN received Class A1 approval for their GPS 155 receiver. GARMIN invited me out to their Kansas headquarters, where chief pilot Doug Carlson briefed me on the approach procedures and then ushered me into the left seat of the company Mooney.

I made a number of GPS approaches that were overlaid on NDB and VOR approaches. As I mentioned in the previous chapter, the first GPS approaches are being overlaid on certain types of ground-based nonprecision approaches; the stand-alone GPS approaches will come later.

One of the important distinctions of a GPS approach is that you must use not only a receiver that has been certified for approaches, but a special database as well. The database includes some waypoints with unique identifiers for GPS approaches.

Not all of these approaches have been charted for GPS as of this writing. However, if the approach is in your database, you can use the chart for the underlying approach. Then ask the controller for, say, the NDB RWY 36 approach and navigate it by means of the GPS receiver.

Your flight path will be the same as if you were using an ADF (except that it will probably be smoother). You must have on board the equipment required for the ground-based navaid—in this case, an ADF receiver; it must be in proper operating condition, but it need not be turned on. (I would turn it on and tune it in anyway, especially if I were in the soup.)

As time goes on, a growing number of charts will be issued that are combined GPS and ground-based approaches. Look at the Corning Municipal approach on the preceding page. It is identified in the upper right corner as being a VOR DME-A approach, with the word "GPS" in parentheses. Two of the IAFs (initial approach fixes) are depicted with four-pointed stars and their identifiers are in parentheses: D016J and D089J. These are waypoints that are not officially designated by the FAA, and as far as your controller is concerned, those waypoints don't exist, but they need to be in the database, along with the one labeled CF (capture fix) 036 and MA (missed approach) 036.

Now let's look at the actual operations you'd perform when shooting a GPS approach, using the GARMIN GPS 155.

The set has an Approach Select page in which the destination airport appears, along with all available GPS approaches. Once you select the desired approach, you are asked to choose the IAF if there is more than one. When the approach has been activated, and the aircraft has proceeded to within 30 nm of the destination airport, you will see the message "Arm Approach Mode." This is done by pressing a remote key labeled APPR. Another message appears, prompting you to enter the destination airport's altimeter setting, which is required for increased lateral precision in the approach mode.

Once the approach mode is armed, the CDI scaling transitions smoothly from 5 nm to 1 nm, and then to .3 nm when you're within 2 nm inbound to the FAF (final approach fix).

The GPS receiver sequences automatically to each waypoint in the selected procedure. Of course, if you are going to do a procedure turn or a holding pattern, you don't want automatic sequencing (it would point you at the next waypoint before you were ready to go there), so you press a remote key labeled GPS SEQ to switch from AUTO to HOLD. In addition to suspending the automatic sequencing function, HOLD puts your CDI or HSI in an OBS mode, causing the needle or deviation bar to provide VOR-type steering information, complete with computer-generated angular deviation (but no scalloping), using as a "phantom VOR" the waypoint that was active when you went to HOLD.

Once you are inbound again, toggle the GPS SEQ key back to AUTO. This gives you continuous distance information to the FAF, and after that, to the MAP (missed approach point). Then, if you want to do a missed approach, press the "Direct To" key and the waypoint coordinates of the missed approach holding point will be displayed. If you want to navigate to the holding point via a specific course, rather than the direct route, put the unit in HOLD and dial the desired course on your CDI or HSI.

Of course, when you are in a radar environment, the controller will usually provide vectors that will set you up for the final approach course. While you are being vectored, select the FAF, put the unit in HOLD, and set up the final approach course on your CDI or HSI. When you intercept the final approach course, switch from HOLD to AUTO and the automatic sequencing will go into effect.

By viewing the position page, you will continually know your distance to the FAF, and, after passing that, to the MAP. Also, you will have good position awareness when you are making a procedure turn or flying a DME arc.

In sum, shooting GPS approaches requires you to use a process that's new in a way, except that it is fundamentally the same as using a flight plan of the type you create in your set for enroute navigation—except that the plan has been created by Jeppesen and resides permanently in the database.

What's more, you have the benefit of *uniformity;* you fly all types of GPS approaches in much the same way, regardless of whether the underlying approaches are VOR, VOR DME, NDB, or RNAV. You use the same instrumentation for all and enjoy GPS's greater precision and stability.

Also, you'll know where you are throughout the approach. As GPS approaches become more commonplace, I expect that we will see fewer of the accidents that result from, say, a pilot tuning in the wrong VOR or the wrong radial. (But even the sophisticated GPS equipment requires proper input, constant monitoring, and full-time alertness. Never, never get complacent!)

GPS nonprecision approaches are here. I can hardly wait for the GPS *precision* approaches!

8

Features to Consider in GPS & Loran Receivers

In this chapter, I will review the major considerations that can help you decide which set is best for you. Note that not all of the functions I will describe are available on all models. Conversely, I have not attempted to describe all features offered by all manufacturers. (The Bendix/King KLN 90 GPS receiver, for example, has over 70 display pages!) To determine which features are found on which models, see the chapter entitled "The GPS, Loran, and Multi-Sensor Models."

True Cost

The true cost of owning a GPS or loran set can go beyond the advertised selling price in several ways.

Updates. Even after you've bought the set, you may be faced with follow-up costs if you want to keep the software up to date. From time to time, a manufacturer will issue new software to improve the performance or provide added capabilities. In most cases, you can expect extra charges for these upgrades.

In some instances, a manufacturer will upgrade your entire set to a more sophisticated model—again, at additional cost. This is particularly applicable these days to IFR certification of GPS receivers. If you have a non-TSOd set, you can expect to have to pay to get it TSOd—if indeed your model *can* be TSOd. (For more details, see the chapter entitled "GPS and Loran for the IFR Pilot.")

For those sets that have user-replaceable databases, updates may be offered every 28 or 56 days by subscription, at an annual cost of about $300 to $600. One-time updates are in the $100-150 area. How often should a database be updated? For strictly VFR flying, once or twice a year may be enough for the pilot who wants to keep his costs down. The IFR pilot will probably opt for the monthly or bimonthly updates—a necessity, in fact, for GPS approach operations. There's also a "paper" update service, offered on a 56-day cycle by Air Chart

System, consisting of a chart of the US and a cumulative listing of all changes; the cost is $40 per year. Contact Air Chart System at 13368 Beach Avenue, Venice, CA 90292; 310-822-1996.

Accessories. Are they included in the basic price or are they extra? For example, some manufacturers of GPS handhelds include such items as cigarette lighter power cables and yoke mounts, while others charge extra or may not supply them at all.

Warranty. The length of warranty can obviously affect the total cost of a set if it requires service. Some manufacturers continue to offer the traditional avionics warranty of one year, while other companies provide warranties of two to three years. ARNAV gives a "lifetime" warranty on certain models, but there is some fine print in that offer.

Dimensions

In many cases, a GPS or loran set will be squeezed into a panel that is already well filled with the traditional nav/comms and other gear, and the size of the box will be an important consideration. Most, but not all, of the current panel-mounted units are a standard 2" high and 6.25" wide. The higher-priced Dzus-rail mount systems that are designed primarily for larger fixed wing aircraft and helicopters have a panel-mounted CDU (control/display unit) of a non-standard size, along with a remote-mounted receiver.

If you're totally out of panel space, there are the portables, which are covered in detail in the chapter appropriately entitled "The GPS Portables."

Display

Type. Many of the lower-priced panel-mounted sets, and all of the handhelds, utilize LCD (liquid crystal display) readouts; they are cheaper, cooler, and draw less power than the other types of display. The downsides are that the characters can be difficult to see at acute viewing angles and the appearance is not as pleasing esthetically as other displays.

Next up the ladder is the vacuum fluorescent display. It is brighter and more attractive than LCD, but has a tendency to wash out in direct sunlight.

The display found most often in the mid- to upper-range models is LED (light-emitting diode), which is bright and very legible.

On the high end of the display spectrum is the CRT (cathode ray tube) that is found, at this writing, on two rather pricey models: Bendix/King's KLN 90B, in monochrome, and Ashtech's Altair AV-12, in color. The CRT offers the type of high resolution that you're accustomed to seeing on your TV screen.

Organization. Since all the available data won't fit into the display window at once, the information is separated into categories, or modes, each of which may have several "pages." For example, the nav mode is likely to contain such data as your present position, range and bearing to a waypoint, desired track, crosstrack error, track angle error, groundspeed, ETE, and more.

Each manufacturer has his own ideas about which items should go together. Ideally, the information you will refer to most often should be on one page, with the less important items on adjoining pages. Some models allow you to customize certain displays by selecting the type of data you want on a given page.

You can determine how the displays of a particular model are organized by examining the operating manual—a useful bit of research that will provide such additional insights as the model's features, ease of use, etc., not to mention the intelligibility of the manual itself.

Factory Database

This is the software that contains pre-programmed lat/lon addresses and other information on airports, navaids, and other waypoints. Like just about everything else, databases vary widely in size, scope, and design. Here are the major criteria:

Coverage area. Most manufacturers offer a choice of geographical coverages. Many sets are available with your choice of either North America, which may also include parts of Central and South America, or an international database that encompasses the rest of the world. For an extra charge, you can get both, if the set has user-replaceable databases.

Types of waypoints. All factory databases contain public use airports and some have military bases as well, for use as a checkpoint or emergency landing facility. In addition, most databases include VORs and NDBs, and some also have intersections. Northstar's database contains victor airways and jet routes; other manufacturers might follow suit in the future.

Waypoint information. All databases provide the waypoint identifier and its lat/lon address. The more sophisticated databases can display a considerable amount of useful airport information, such as its city of location; radio frequencies; runway IDs, lengths, and surface; lighting; and type of instrument approach. Some sets even allow you to insert a comment, such as WATCH FOR MOOSE AT NORTH END OF RWY or DONT ORDER THE VICHYSSOISE AT DENNYS.

Method of Updating. It is desirable to update the database from time to time, to incorporate changes in frequencies, identifiers, navaid locations, etc. The lowest cost receivers have internal databases and must be returned to the factory or a dealer for a computer chip replacement. The more sophisticated receivers have user-replaceable databases encased in data cards or cartridges that can easily be exchanged on a one-time or subscription basis. Another option offered by a growing number of manufacturers is updating via a computer disk and a cable that connects your PC to your receiver. (This is less convenient than swapping data cards, but it should also be less expensive.)

User Waypoints. These are waypoints that you enter; they might include such locations as a private landing strip, a scenic spot you want to revisit, or a route that will keep you clear of special use airspace. Some pilots enter waypoints that will set them up for approaches at often-used airports at night or during reduced visibility—but I must emphasize that it is neither legal nor safe to shoot a homemade approach when conditions are below VFR minimums.

All models allow you to define a user waypoint by either entering its latitude and longitude coordinates or by pressing a key that will automatically store the coordinates of your present position. In addition, most sets let you define a waypoint by entering its bearing and distance from a waypoint that is already in the database.

Some models can store as many as 1,000 or 2,000 user waypoints, which is far more waypoints than most pilots will ever need.

Ease of Waypoint Access. Some models are limited to a numeric system for the labeling of user waypoints, which means that you'll probably have to create a directory to help you remember, for example, that you stored an approach to Runway 14 at Beaver Municipal as Waypoint #35. Other models allow you to enter up to a 5-digit name, such as BVR14.

In the factory database, waypoints are stored by their identifiers, so in some models you will have to know that Beaver's ID is Q44. The more sophisticated units spare you the chore of looking up the ID by allowing you to dial in the waypoint name or the city in which it is located; before you've finished dialing, the computer will usually recognize the waypoint you want.

Navigation Features

Since your inherent reason for using a GPS or loran set is to get from place to place, the chances are you'll be using the navigation mode most often. Virtually every unit will compute and display the bearing and distance to the waypoint to which you are navigating, as well as your groundspeed, ETE (plus ETA if it's equipped with an internal clock), and the lat/lon of your present position.

An electronic CDI is displayed to keep you on course. Other forms of steering information can include digital readouts of the actual track being flown; the desired track (the direct courseline computed between the FROM and TO waypoints); and the crosstrack error, computed to the nearest tenth or hundredth of a nautical mile.

Incidentally, if you wander too far to suit the computer, it may flash an OFF COURSE message on the screen, embarrassing you in front of your passengers. (Oh, well, you can always tell them it was a sightseeing excursion.)

Here are some other types of navigation information, not all of which are found in all sets.

Flight plan. Sometimes referred to also as a route plan, a flight plan is a programmed trip of at least two legs, although most models can compute flight plans consisting of many legs. But since GPS and loran navigation enables you to fly directly to your destination, why should you want a multi-leg flight plan? Well, there will be times when it may be necessary or desirable to dog-leg because of special use airspace, terrain, weather, air traffic control requirements, or just plain sightseeing.

The flight plan feature can significantly reduce pilot workload. When you arrive at the destination waypoint of the leg you are using, an automatic waypoint sequencing function will activate the next one. Some sets also have a turn anticipation function that advises you of the new heading in time to avoid overshooting it.

In most models, the flight plan can be easily reversed for the return trip. And the majority of units will store a number of flight plans, which is especially handy if you fly the same routes on a regular basis.

Remote ranging. Most sets will display the bearing and distance from your present position to a waypoint other than the one to which you are navigating, in case you need to deviate because of weather, fuel, etc. But not all units will perform the additional function I call remote ranging—and please note that each manufacturer has his own name for this feature. Remote ranging computes the bearing and distance between any two selected waypoints, not necessarily related to your current route of flight; this is useful for flight planning. Some sets have the additional ability to display radio frequencies and other information relative to those waypoints.

Nearest waypoint. This is sometimes referred to as an emergency search function. If the engine coughs, or a passenger expresses an urgent need, the press of a button or two will display the bearing, distance, and other information regarding the airport nearest to your present position. Some models give you the choice of more than one nearby airport, since the very closest field may not be the most suitable. And certain models will also display the nearest VORs, NDBs, and intersections.

There is a non-emergency benefit to this function: you can easily keep track of your position along your route of flight by referring to your bearing and distance to a nearby airport or navaid.

Of course, the set must have the airports and navaids resident in a database in order to utilize this function.

Special Use Airspace Alert. This is another function that is found, to one degree or another, on most models that have databases. The set will have in permanent memory the locations and shapes of SUAs. A warning message will appear on the screen if you are close to or inside the airspace. Some sets will also display the frequency of the controlling agency, to make it easy for you to call for a clearance through the airspace if desired. The types of SUA that are included will vary, with the more sophisticated sets alerting you to the proximity of Class B and C airspace; MOAs; and Prohibited, Restricted, and Alert Areas.

Minimum safe altitude. For this feature, the computer has in memory an altitude map that is programmed with sectors similar to those on the NOS sectional charts. The set's display gives a digital readout of the highest obstruction—plus an extra thousand feet or so of safety margin—of the sector the aircraft is navigating in. A companion feature, called minimum enroute safe altitude, provides the same obstruction information between the aircraft and its destination waypoint.

A drawback to the MSA/MESA function is that it will often display higher obstructions than you will actually encounter. That's because the sectors are quite large—60 nm in a north-south direction by about 40 to 50 nm in an east-west direction. So if, for example, the highest obstruction in a given sector is a 6,000-foot mountain, then 7,000 feet might be displayed as your minimum safe altitude even if that mountain is miles away from your route of flight.

VNAV. The acronym stands for vertical navigation guidance, a function that is most commonly used to create a sort of do-it-yourself glideslope from cruising altitude down to the altitude of a waypoint such as an approach fix, traffic pattern entry point, etc. The use of VNAV gives you a smooth descent without the likelihood of abrupt power reductions or last-minute ear-popping plunges.

With most sets, you program the altitude you want to attain when you arrive at the waypoint, along with the desired angle or rate of descent. Descent guidance is provided in the form of a digital display of the desired altitude. To stay "on glideslope," simply keep your altimeter matched to the digital display.

In addition to descent guidance, VNAV can provide a climb profile—for example, as an aid in transitioning smoothly to a higher MEA (minimum enroute altitude).

Winds aloft. Since the computer knows your course and groundspeed, it can calculate a wind triangle if you enter the true airspeed and heading (or if you have an air/data computer that provides the input automatically). Your local FSS or Flight Watch specialist will thank you for including this information in your pilot reports.

Parallel offset. This function allows you to fly a track that is parallel to the direct route between waypoints. Not all manufacturers agree that this is a valuable function, and I, for one, feel that its use can cause confusion in the cockpit if the pilot forgets that he has it activated.

Moving map displays. This fascinating navigation tool is arousing an ever-increasing amount of interest, and I'm going to devote a fairish amount of space to describe it properly.

A moving map display gives you graphic awareness of your position at all times. It is essentially an electronic chart that shows your plane's current position in relationship to waypoints such as airports, VORs, NDBs, and intersections.

You can choose from a number of scales; it's somewhat like switching electronically from a WAC chart to a sectional to a terminal area chart, except that the moving map system's computer gives you a much broader range—often from a fraction of a mile to several hundred miles.

Most systems provide a choice of map orientations: north up, ground track up, or heading up.

There's a symbol on the screen representing your airplane, and you can see Hometown Airport coming up at your two o'clock position, and just ahead is the VOR.

In other words, you don't have to interpolate your position on a paper chart from information provided by your nav receiver. The electronic chart shows you where you are all the time—even as you're taxiing out to the active runway!

In an enroute mode of a typical display, the aircraft symbol remains stationary while other symbols depicting airports and navaids slide by. Switch to an approach or arrival mode and the destination airport symbol holds still while the airplane symbol emulates your flight path toward it. You can actually see the little symbolic plane making a downwind leg, then turning base and final—lined up on the runway as precisely (or imprecisely) as your real airplane.

Some systems depict special use airspace, so you can use the device as a visual aid in skirting around a no-no area such as a Class B airspace.

How does the moving map know where you are? It gets your position information from an interface with a GPS or loran sensor. And its own database stores the locations of the airports, navaids, etc.

Some moving map systems are stand-alone panel-mounted units, others utilize portable computers as displays, and the most recent devices are handheld and panel-mounted GPS receivers with built-in moving map displays.

Let's look at the pros and cons of each type.

In general, panel-mounted equipment has the brighter display of the CRT (cathode ray tube) in contrast, so to speak, with the simpler LCD (liquid crystal display) that's universally used in the portables because of its low power consumption.

Panel space permitting, the panel-mount's map display can be placed directly in the pilot's line of vision. And controls that are fixed in the panel may be easier to operate than those of portable equipment. Installed equipment is neater and tends to be classier looking.

On the minus side, panel-mounted avionics have a higher price tag, to which must be added the cost of installation. In addition, available panel space is likely to impose some restriction on the size of the display.

(On the subject of display size, I should note that I have an Argus 5000 panel-mounted system in my plane and have also flown with the GARMIN 95 and Apollo 920 portables, all of which have rather small displays. While larger is undoubtedly better, these diminutive displays have not posed a real problem for me, and I am a long-time member of the bifocal set. The trick is to use fairly small range settings—40 nm or less, depending on the density of the area—and deselect any symbols you don't really need.)

Portable equipment offers greater utility in that it can be taken easily from plane to plane (or boat, backpack, etc.). If a personal computer is being used as the control/display unit, it will, of course, be available for all its other PC functions. And depending on the computer, you may have the benefit of a large display.

Portables are self-powered and thus will continue to function (for as long as the batteries hold out) in the event of a failure of the aircraft's electrical system.

A significant downside, depending on cockpit space, could be the placement of a computer where it could be readily viewed and operated by the pilot. (Handheld GPS receivers with yoke-mounted brackets don't pose this problem.)

Signal Acquisition

Number of GPS channels. GPS receivers are equipped with one to twelve channels, depending on the manufacturer's design philosophy. Conventional wisdom might say "the more channels, the better," since a single-channel receiver works by sequencing rapidly through all satellites in view, while an eight-channel unit, for example, can track up to eight satellites simultaneously. But that's an oversimplification, since other aspects of the receiver design come into play, and a well-engineered set with one channel could function very effectively.

Loran chain reception. Some loran receivers are capable of receiving only one chain at a time, either automatically or by pilot selection. Others have multi-chain capability, meaning they can track a number of stations from two or more chains simultaneously and automatically select the best chains and stations. Most of the IFR-certifiable sets perform multi-chain tracking.

ASF correction. Additional secondary (phase) factor is a reference to the amount of delay in the speed of a transmitted loran signal as it travel over land versus sea water. For optimum accuracy, this must be compensated for, and the situation is complicated by the fact that ground conductivity varies from area to area. Some manufacturers test for conductivity at many sites and incorporate the results in the loran set's memory.

Some units allow the pilot to further compensate for inaccuracies by entering small ASF corrections. This is normally done when the aircraft has been taxied to a spot on an airport where the exact lat/lon coordinates are known.

Automatic mag/var correction. This function, found on most GPS and loran sets, compensates for local magnetic variation, in order to properly reference the various nav displays to magnetic headings.

Some models are programmed to account for the slight changes in magnetic variation that occur from year to year. In addition, certain units have provision for a manual mag/var setting to allow users to navigate by true headings—for example, in aerial survey work.

Data Port

Most models have a serial data port, which is a computer connection that allows the set to interface with a compatible moving map display, fuel computer, or other peripheral.

Training

Strictly speaking, this is not a feature of the receiver, but it's important that you consider the quality of the training you will receive in the use of the model you select. The many functions available in your GPS or loran set are wasted if you don't know how to use them properly.

How effective is the set's user manual? Is it written in pilot's terms or arcane engineering-ese? Are the various functions organized and explained in a logical manner, related to the way they will actually be used?

Alas, the user manuals often are far more poorly designed and produced than the receivers themselves, and you'll be fortunate if the set you choose has been blessed with a good user's guide.

Some sets have a training mode that enables you to take a simulated flight in the comfort of your home, where you will be able to concentrate on what the knobs and buttons do without the distraction of impacting a mass of aluminum or rock.

Finally, you should expect to receive ample training from the dealer who sells you the system. In addition to one-on-one instruction, some dealers conduct classes and seminars, often in cooperation with the manufacturers.

Now let's take a look at the models themselves, starting with the panel-mounted GPS, loran, and multi-sensor systems.

9

Panel-Mounted GPS, Loran & Multi-Sensor Models

Let me confess that I spent a considerable amount of time deciding how to present the models in a way that would make some organizational sense. The marketplace has become a hodge-podge of stand-alone GPS units, stand-alone lorans, lorans with optional remote GPS sensors, GPS and loran in the same box, and so on.

What seems to work best is to put all the panel-mounted GPS and loran variants into one gigantic chapter, listed by manufacturer. The GPS portables follow in a separate chapter.

I've led off with those companies that I consider to be the heavy hitters, in terms of consumer acceptance and high-caliber products. (The two usually go hand in hand.)

This chapter contains the major features and specifications of all the panel-mounted units that are currently manufactured as of this writing. Unless otherwise noted, the dimensions are the standard 2" high by approximately 6.25" wide.

I've been able to fly and evaluate some, but not all, of the models. The reports on those that I have had hands-on experience with are labeled, appropriately, "Hands-On Evaluation." They include my personal comments, and are longer than the others. This is not to suggest that the others are less worthy of your consideration.

Chances are you'll make your buying decision based on a combination of features, price, and user-friendliness. The last is subjective, and before you buy, you'd be well advised to get a good demonstration and make sure the model you're interested in really suits your personality.

Now, here are the models.

II Morrow

I think of Ray Morrow as the Henry Ford of the loran manufacturing industry. He and the company he founded, II Morrow (yes, it was the second Morrow enterprise), really popularized loran by providing the first practical-size receiver—2" high by 6.25" wide—at a practical price. For an encore, II Morrow introduced the Flybrary,™ which was the first factory database produced for general aviation avionics.

Flushed with success, the company cranked out a succession of loran models, each with its own particular collection of features, but there was no orderly sequence; for instance, the consumer could not buy a top-of-the-line model that had all of the desirable features.

But II Morrow has now gotten its act a little more organized, with a budget Flybuddy line of GPS receivers and a more sophisticated 2001 series that provides GPS as a stand-alone unit or in combination with a loran sensor and a fuel/air data system. (Note: The functions of a fuel/air data system are described in the reports on II Morrow's 2001 series and Trimble's TNL 3000T.)

The **Flybuddy GPS** has an 8-channel sensor and comes in three flavors: 820, 820R, and 820C, which differ only in the content of their respective databases; more on that shortly.

The introduction of the Flybuddy series signaled a departure from the familiar II Morrow face consisting of two concentric control knobs, six pushbuttons, and a large rectangular LED display. Instead, we still see the familiar concentric knobs, but they are flanked by two large buttons and six small ones, as well as a half-dozen annunciation lights. On the left side, the display is smaller than before, but has a higher character capacity (32) than previous II Morrow models.

And in place of II Morrow's customary LED display is a supertwist LCD readout, which is backlit all the time; the contrast can be adjusted by the dealer to improve legibility. Each display page has two lines of dot matrix characters.

At the top of the Flybuddy box is a slot for a data card, applicable to the 820R and 820C versions.

Let's take a closer look at the controls. There are four mode buttons: NAV, DB, FP, and SYS.

The Navigation Mode

Pressing the NAV button calls up the navigation pages. The outer Control knob and the inner Data knob are used to select the desired page. One of the nav pages shows bearing and distance to the waypoint on the first line and a CDI (course deviation indicator) on the second line. The CDI is rather sophisticated, and its sensitivity depends on whether you are more than a mile or less than a mile off course. If you are to the left of course, your off-course distance is displayed on the left side and a trend arrow is shown at the right. Also, deviation bars radiate from the right of a symbolic airplane in the center. The trend arrow indicates whether you are correcting or going farther afield. If you then move to the right of course, the digital distance readout will jump to the right side of the display and the trend arrow will hop to the left. This is a little disconcerting at first, but at least it keeps you on your toes, and possibly on course as well.

The CDI is included on another nav page, along with bearing to the waypoint and actual track. Among the other nav displays are: desired track, ETE (estimated time enroute), elapsed flight time, and the next waypoint of a flight plan.

The Database Mode

The basic 820 has an internal database consisting of airports and VORs worldwide. The only information provided is the waypoint's lat/lon and, in the case of airports, fuel availability.

The 820R and 820C versions have regional and continental data cards in addition to the internal database. The data cards provide frequency and runway information; NDBs; and intersections, heliports, and seaplane bases on some of the cards.

Geographical coverage for the 820R consists of a choice of eastern or western North America. The 820C covers the entire US, Canada,

The Flybuddy is available with or without a user-replaceable database..

and Mexico. An international version, encompassing the world except for North America, is also available.

All Flybuddy models have memory for up to 100 user waypoints, which can be defined by lat/lon or present position, but not by radial and distance from an existing waypoint. Unlike some sets that require you to name a waypoint before defining it, the Flybuddy automatically assigns an identification number to a vacant waypoint slot. You can continue to use that number, or change it at your leisure to a more easily remembered name containing up to six characters.

The Flybuddy does not offer the third method available in many other sets: defining a waypoint by its radial and distance from an existing waypoint.

A customer comment can be stored for each user waypoint, as well as for each flight plan.

Navigating to a Waypoint

Let's try a little basic navigation with the Flybuddy. Say you want to fly directly to a waypoint. We'll think big and head for San Francisco International Airport. Press the Direct (D with an arrow through it) button and if necessary, turn the Control knob to select the airport database. Then, by using the Control and Data knobs, dial in S, F, and O and press the ENT (enter) button. This gets you the nav information described earlier—bearing, distance, CDI, etc. You can bypass the process of dialing the identifier by scrolling to the desired waypoint , then pressing the Direct and ENT keys.

Incidentally, it's a good idea to put into the user section your home base airport and other airports you fly to often, even though they are in the airport database, because it's easier to retrieve them for navigation purposes by scrolling through the small user section than by dialing in their identifiers one letter at a time. Also, you can insert pertinent information, such as a radio frequency, field elevation, etc., using the custom comment function, which is not available for the airport database

On your way to SFO, will the Flybuddy inform you of the presence of the San Francisco Class B airspace? No, it does not have an SUA alert function.

The database waypoints closest to your present position are readily available. Press the NAV button twice (or just once if you're in the NAV mode), and the first display you'll see will be the identifier, bearing, and distance to the nearest airport, along with an arrow pointing in its general direction. Turning the Data knob calls up the same information for each of the next nine nearest airports, then the five nearest VORs, followed by the five nearest user waypoints.

The Flight Plan Mode

The Flybuddy allows you to store 10 flight plans with up to 10 legs apiece, which is a considerable improvement over earlier II Morrow models that offered only one flight plan. What's more, you can give each of the Flybuddy's flight plans a name, and you can insert one custom comment for each flight plan.

Incidentally, you can create a sort of mini flight plan in the NAV mode. One of the NAV pages shows the waypoint you're navigating from and the waypoint you're going to, and you can program in an additional waypoint, which is displayed as NEXT. When you arrive at your TO waypoint, the Flybuddy automatically sequences to the NEXT waypoint, which becomes the new TO waypoint, and then you can add a new NEXT waypoint, and so on.

The System Mode

The following functions can be adjusted by the user in the system mode, which is activated by pressing the SYS button:

An Auto Nav Scroll function causes most of the NAV pages to appear in constant rotation at pilot-selectable intervals of one to nine seconds.

A waypoint arrival alert can be set for distances ranging from 0.1 nm to 9.99 nm. There is also a countdown timer settable for one second less than 100 hours, which is a lot longer than I care to fly at one sitting. The alert light will activate when the timer reaches zero. (Because of the display update rate, the timer display skips every third digit during countdown.)

The CDI sensitivity can be set for values ranging from 0.01 to 1.99 nm per mark.

A security system allows you to enter your name and other information, such as your address and phone number.

Satellite status information is also found in the system mode.

My Impressions

During my flight evaluation, the LCD display was really put to the test in its location at the far right side of a Warrior panel. Many LCDs are virtually illegible when viewed from an extreme side angle, but the Flybuddy's display comes through loud and clear. However, I also viewed a unit that was installed in the bottom section of a helicopter console, and the display was not readable at that low spot.

The Flybuddy is quite straightforward in its operation, and the learning curve for the use of the pushbutton and knob controls was relatively quick. Every GPS manufacturer who wants to offer a variety of features must face the problem of making these functions accessible to the user via a system of knobs and/or buttons that won't be overly confusing. II Morrow has provided a good solution in the Flybuddy design. I should add that the company has come a long way since the early Flybrary models with their cumbersome database regions.

The user manual is a lot better than the diminutive document provided for the 920 handheld. It comes in a 3-ring binder, the pages are 5½" x 8½", and there are plenty of illustrations. However, some of the functions are not described as completely as they could be.

All in all, the Flybuddy is a moderately priced unit that offers intelligent, easy-to-use operation. The LCD display is not bad, but not as nice as the LED technology used on their higher-priced models. The standard internal database is very limited; the optional data cards, though more complete, do not contain any special use airspace, and thus the set cannot warn you if you are about to trespass into verboten territory.

Prices: $2,495 for the 820; $2,795 for the 820R; and $2,995 for the 820C.

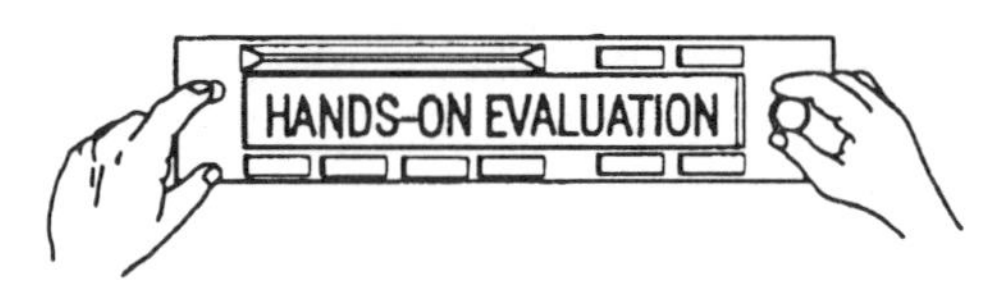

The **2001 GPS** traces its heritage to a building block concept, introduced by II Morrow in 1991, called the NMS (Navigation Management System). The heart of the system is an NMC, which, as you might guess, stands for Nav Management Computer. The NMC looks for all the world like a high-tech GPS or loran receiver, but you might say it is neither, or either, or both.

It is a black box—very black, quite handsome, and complete with the expected control knobs, pushbuttons, a display area, and a slot for a data card. Nestling inside is a smart computer and everything else

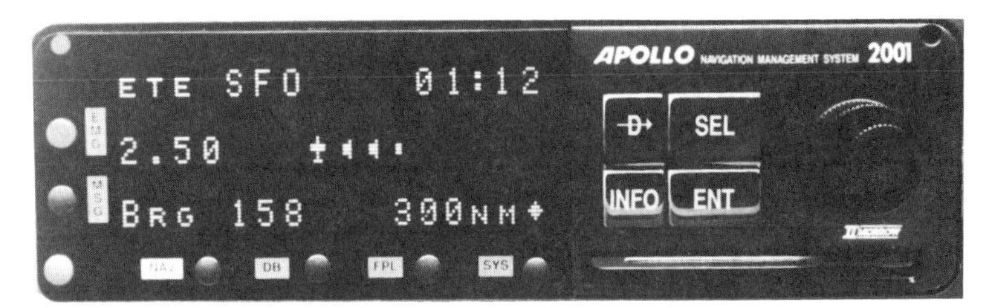

The 2001 is available as a stand-alone GPS receiver or as a multi-sensor system that also includes a remote loran and/or air/data system.

you'd need for a sophisticated nav receiver—except for a sensor of any kind.

II Morrow's idea was to allow the customer to decide, by installing remote-mounted sensors, whether he or she wanted a loran receiver, a GPS receiver, or a multi-sensor system capable of both loran and GPS navigation. The customer could also add a fuel/air data system, and, in fact, the NMS architecture is designed to support up to 255 remote sensors!

Well, the idea seemed to make a lot of sensing—'scuse me, *sense*—but as GPS began to overshadow loran, it became clear that a lot of customers wanted GPS capability and it would save cost as well as behind-the-panel space to build a GPS sensor into the NMC and offer it as a stand-alone GPS receiver.

So that's what II Morrow did, and that's what the 2001 GPS is. You can still add a remote-mounted loran sensor and/or a fuel/air data system, so the building block concept remains, except that you start with a GPS receiver as the foundation. (The sensor-less NMC is available as well.)

The 2001 GPS has an 8-channel sensor (the original NMS sensor was 5-channel). The optional loran sensor is multi-chain and master-independent; it can track two chains and up to 12 stations.

With the loran sensor installed, the system is TSOd to C60b and C115a. At this writing, the 2001 GPS does not have TSO C129. II Morrow will seek Class A1 approval. The cost of upgrading will be $1,200.

Beauty That No Longer Glares

As I mentioned earlier, the box itself is very good-looking; it resembles a high-tech auto stereo set. Originally, all this beauty came smack into the eye of the beholder—literally—in the form of reflected glare from the display in conditions of direct sunlight. II Morrow has provided a fix in the form of a redesigned filter, which is on the newer units and available for earlier models as a retrofit.

The Controls

There are four small round mode buttons running horizontally along the bottom, for displaying nav, database, flight plan, and system pages. On the left side, vertically, are three more round buttons. A red one (all the others are black) instantly calls up the nearest airport identifier, along with bearing, distance, and II Morrow's clever arrow that actually points in the direction to turn. Below that is a button whose annunciator will flash if there's a warning or other message for you to read. Below that is the power button.

The other controls consist of four rectangular keys and two concentric knobs, for entry or retrieval of information and additional functions. It may sound a little complex, but it's really quite straightforward.

The display is LED dot matrix, with three lines of highly legible yellow alphanumerics.

Take a Card

You get a choice of data cards. The North America card covers the 50 states, Canada, the Caribbean, Mexico, Central America, and South America. The international card encompasses all parts of the globe except North and South America. Included in the database are airports, VORs, NDBs, and intersections. Airport information includes identifier; city, state, and country; radio frequencies; runway direction, length, surface, and lighting; fuel availability; and types of instrument approaches.

Waypoints can be accessed by identifier, facility name, or city. Up to 200 user waypoints can be stored. These can be defined by lat/lon, radial and distance from a known waypoint, or present position.

You can enter a custom comment for any waypoint or flight plan—for example, KEY UNICOM 5 TIMES FOR LIGHTS. As many as 100 comment pages of up to 48 characters each can be stored.

And there is storage space for 10 flight plans of up to 20 legs apiece.

Lots of Features

The 2001 GPS has other features we've come to look for in sophisticated equipment of this type, including special use airspace alerts; minimum safe altitude display; VNAV; and a search function for the 20 nearest airports, VORs, NDBs, intersections, user waypoints, and special use airspaces. The airport search can be customized according to a specified minimum runway length, type of surface, and whether or not lighted.

An optional ($495) Apollo altitude encoder provides such amenities as altitude alert, enhanced VNAV, and a 3-D special use airspace capability that won't trigger an alert if, for example, you are flying above the ceiling of a Class B airspace.

A function called Search Around a Waypoint allows you to select any waypoint in the database and then look up the 20 nearest waypoints in that category; this can be useful in flight planning.

Then there's II Morrow's unique Auto Nav feature that causes the navigation pages to scroll at a selectable rate. Also, up to seven nav pages can be customized as to their content.

FF/AD

The fuel flow/air data option uses sophisticated equipment developed by Shadin, the company that manufacturers the popular Digiflo and Miniflo fuel computers. The fuel flow portion of the FF/AD will compute the rate of fuel consumption, fuel used, fuel remaining, range, fuel needed to all waypoints of the active flight plan, and fuel remaining at each waypoint (based, of course, on the current rate of consumption and groundspeed). There is even a function that warns you that in so many minutes you will start to dip into your fuel reserve; you can select the amount of warning time as well as the quantity of reserve.

Air data information is something many corporate pilots have enjoyed in their pricey equipment. Now it's available for general aviation at moderate cost as a result of this option. Basically, the air data system automatically provides you with useful information that you would otherwise have to compute with manual input—for example: true air temperature, true airspeed, density altitude, wind speed, and magnetic and true wind direction. It all shows up on the NMS display with no workload on your part.

In order to utilize this sensor, your aircraft must be equipped with a heading instrument—such as a CDI, HSI, or DG—that has synchro output (sometimes referred to as bootstrap).

Other features of the 2001 GPS include a flight timer that can be set to initiate on power-up or at any desired groundspeed, and a countdown timer.

Fly it at Home

The set has a fully operational simulator mode. This feature allows you to plug in a groundspeed, altitude, and flight plan, and "fly" the trip of your choice. Since you can utilize virtually all of the set's functions, the simulator mode is good for training purposes and also enables you to create flight plans in the comfort of your home. A 110V AC power supply is included with the unit.

To assess its ease of use, I put the unit through its paces before reading through the fat user manual (do not try this while flying an airplane!) and found that I was able to use most of its functions without too much stumbling.

It is always a challenge to design the controls and architecture of a multi-featured, computerized piece of equipment that will fit in a relatively small space and yet not be overly complicated to use. I believe that II Morrow has done this very well. The system has been designed with intelligence and with the user in mind.

The user manual is comprehensive and generally well written. Unfortunately, it perpetuates an annoying weakness I have found in other II Morrow manuals: a tendency to refer the user to another part of the manual for further information without explaining how to get there. Go to the index for help and you may or may not get it.

All in all, II Morrow has done a very creditable job in designing a sophisticated nav system with a host of useful functions.

In its stand-alone form, the 2001 GPS lists for $3,995. With the remote loran sensor added, the price is $5,495. The further addition of the fuel/air data system brings the tab to $8,495 or $8,795, depending on the aircraft engine.

Dzus-rail mount versions are available, at prices ranging from $6,495 to $12,995, according to configuration.

Note: II Morrow's 920 handheld is covered in the next chapter.

Trimble

Trimble Navigation was founded by Charles Trimble, formerly an engineer with Hewlett-Packard. When H-P, which had been conducting considerable research and development of loran and GPS, decided not to proceed with manufacturing this equipment, Trimble acquired the technology—initially for the marine market and then for aviation as well. Trimble manufactures GPS receivers and a multi-sensor system, but no stand-alone loran model.

The **TNL-3000T** is Trimble's multi-sensor system. Unlike other systems that have at least one of the sensors remotely mounted, the TNL-3000T has both the GPS and loran sensors encased in its standard-size 2" H x 6.25" W x 10.8" D box. The Trimble approach should save a bit on installation costs, in addition to helping minimize the maze of wires and hardware crammed behind the panel.

The TNL-3000T replaces the TNL-3000. The latter is certifiable under TSOs C60b and C115a, meaning that you can have the unit certified for enroute and terminal operations, using the loran sensor as the primary nav system. The newer model is certifiable under C129 as well, so GPS can also be used as the primary source. At this writing, it's Class A2, but Trimble is going for A1 and may have it by the time you read this. The cost of upgrading will be no more than the difference in list price between the present model and the upgraded one.

The GPS receiver is 6-channel and the loran receiver is multi-chain master-independent. The latter features a digital signal processing design that, according to the manufacturer, provides extreme signal sensitivity and superior interference rejection.

You can manually choose either GPS or loran. More likely, you will prefer to select AUTO and let the set's computer make the decision. On orders from the Trimble management, which, as previously noted, is biased toward GPS, the computer starts out on the assumption that the satellite signals are paramount. However, during the flight it constantly compares GPS's position solution to that of loran, and will switch to the latter if that turns out to be providing better position information. An annunciation of either "GPS" or "LORAN" tells you which system is in use, but for all practical purposes it hardly matters, since most of the set's features operate in the same way regardless.

The TNL-3000T's display is LED with two lines of dot matrix alphanumerics. The unit is controlled by nine function keys and two concentric knobs. Along the bottom of the box are six mode keys: NAV, WPT, FPL, CALC, AUX, and APT/VOR. Also on the bottom of the case is a slot that houses the Jeppesen NavData data card. Running vertically along the right side of the display are three function keys: D (direct), MSG, and ENT. To the right of these keys are the two selector knobs.

You get a choice of North American or international data cards. Updates are available on a 28-day subscription basis at costs ranging from $495 to $925 per year.

There is memory for 250 user waypoints, which can be defined by present position, lat/lon, or bearing and distance from an existing waypoint.

Press the WPT key and a waypoint page of a certain category—for example, airport—will appear on the display. You can then call up the particular airport you want by pressing the ENT key and then using the knobs to dial up the airport's three-digit identifier. (Mercifully, Trimble's North American database does not use the international four-letter identifiers for the US airports, as do those manufacturers who require you to laboriously dial in a "K" as the first letter of each and every federally designated airport.) If you don't know the identifier, you can instead dial the name of the airport or city in which it is located.

Once you have the airport you want, use the outer knob to access the various pages of information: airport city and name; radio frequencies; field elevation; runway direction, length, width, surface, and traffic pattern direction (nice!); also, if applicable, lighting, IFR approach(es), and services.

To minimize page-turning, in some cases the information will travel across the display, sort of like the stock market ticker at your favorite broker, if indeed you still have a favorite broker.

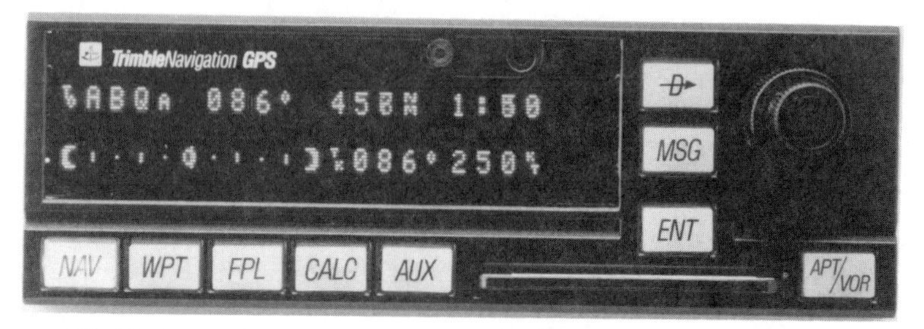

The TNL-3000 has both the loran and GPS sensors encased in the panel-mounted box.

To get to the VOR category, press WPT again, and so on, for NDBs, intersections, and user waypoints. Here's another nice touch: a page showing the Morse code for the VOR or NDB identifier—a useful aid in verifying that you've got the right station tuned in on your VOR or ADF receiver.

To access the 20 nearest waypoints, press the APT/VOR key until the waypoint category is displayed, then turn the outer selector knob to page through the information on that waypoint. You can navigate to any one of the 20 nearest airports by pressing the "direct" key.

Have it Your Way

The TNL-3000T has six half-pages of nav information, as follows: bearing, distance, and ETE to the current destination waypoint; CDI, track, and groundspeed; track and MAINTAIN ODD (or EVEN altitude, based on track); ETE and ETA; desired track, actual track, and digital course correction; and MSA and MESA (minimum safe altitude and minimum enroute safe altitude, similar to the sectors displayed on aeronautical charts).

Since the set's display has space for two lines of data, you can customize your nav display by putting any two of the above half-pages together, one atop the other. This is done by means of the concentric knobs. Also, a VNAV profile can be displayed on the bottom line of a nav page, once the VNAV function becomes active.

Lots More Features

Up to 20 flight plans of 20 legs each can be stored. When you are approaching a flight plan leg that will require a heading change of more than 10 degrees, a turn anticipation function will let you know when to turn and to what heading.

An alert function provides an advisory message you if you are going to penetrate (or are inside of) any type of special use airspace. The appropriate controlling agency and radio frequency is also displayed. You can disable the advisory for any or all airspace categories.

If unexpected weather, fuel condition, etc., causes you to consider an alternate destination, you can display any other airport's bearing, distance, and ETE directly below the bearing, distance, and ETE of your current destination. This is a handy way of reviewing your options.

Pressing the CALC key puts you in the calculator mode, for such E-6B computations as time, distance and speed; fuel management, pressure and density altitude; true airspeed, and winds aloft. Some manual inputs are necessary for these computations unless you have the set interfaced with Shadin's F/ADC fuel/air data system; more on that shortly.

There is also a crosswind and headwind calculation for the runway you will be using; this requires manual input of the runway ID and the wind direction and velocity.

CALC also gets you to the VNAV page; you can set up a descent or ascent profile in feet per minute or degrees.

To store your present position, push CALC twice.

And here's yet another feature not normally found in this type of equipment: press AUX to see as many as 10 programmable checklists of up to 26 entries apiece.

An anti-theft function, when enabled, will prevent the set from operating until a code is entered. Use the factory code or create your own. You can also use this code to cause a display with your name and aircraft tail number (or any other message) to appear when the unit is turned on.

A dead reckoning/demo mode allows you to program a simulated flight at home, complete with selected groundspeed, departure point, flight plan, and other functions. The set will simulate the flight, providing all the information you would receive on a real trip, including nearest waypoints, special use airspace advisories, VNAV, etc. The mode can also be activated for dead reckoning during flight, provided the unit is not receiving signals that are adequate for a position fix.

My Impressions

At this writing, the TNL-3000T has been installed in my Tiger for quite awhile, along with Shadin's F/ADC fuel/air data system. The latter is a remote-mounted box with sensors that enables the Trimble unit to display true airspeed, pressure and density altitude, true outside air temperature, and winds aloft—all automatically, without any pilot input. With a fuel transducer as part of the system, the F/ADC functions as a fuel flow sensor and the TNL-3000T displays the following: fuel flow rate; fuel required to reach the destination waypoint; fuel remaining; fuel efficiency, in nautical miles per gallon; absolute range; range remaining; fuel on board at arrival; fuel reserve at arrival; time reserve at arrival; and total fuel used.

In addition, the F/ADC provides automatic altitude input for GPS navigation when only three satellites are in view.

Together, the TNL-3000T and the F/ADC provide a very effective flight management system. The F/ADC lists for $2,550, and is available for other GPS and loran receivers as well. I strongly recommend that if you decide on this installation, you have it done by an avionics shop that has already gone through what is apparently a rather intense learning curve; you don't want to be the first one on the operating table.

The TNL-3000T is a well designed, highly capable navigation system and it has served me almost flawlessly. The only place where I have lost a signal (and that has been momentarily) has occurred at a spot notoriously overpowered by a military installation—unfortunately, on the final approach path to an airport.

As you can readily see from the laundry list cited earlier, the set is chock-full of features, most of them intelligently thought out and some of them unique to the TNL-3000T.

Trimble has made some meaningful software improvements since the original model was introduced. One learning curve faced by many manufacturers has been in the design of user-friendly flight planning—especially the editing of an active flight plan. When you have to make a sudden change in your route because of weather, an ATC clearance, etc., you don't want to be confronted with obscure computer logic in your nav system.

Trimble's original flight planning architecture was less than easy to work with. It is now somewhat better, but I wish it were even more straightforward. That is my only substantial quibble about a generally excellent system.

Well, actually, I've got another one. The user manual is very comprehensive and reasonably well organized, but still I had to call the factory for answers to about a dozen questions. Oh, well, my comment that "nothing's perfect" certainly applies to user manuals. (And to this writer, as well.)

Quibbles aside, the TNL-3000T is a super navigator. There's nothing like having both GPS and loran at your disposal, especially in a set that will automatically select the system that is providing the best position information at any given time.

In my opinion, the set offers just about everything you could reasonably expect in its price range.

Price: $5,245, not including loran antenna. The older non-TSOd TNL-3000 (which is no longer being manufactured) can be upgraded to a TNL-3000T at the factory, at a cost of $750. Note that it will then require a data card configured especially for the TSOd system.

The **TNL 3100T** is a Dzus-rail mount version of the TNL-3000T. Price: $9,745.

The **TNL-2000A** is a GPS-only unit. It is equivalent to the TNL-3000, minus the loran capability. Price: $3,995. The **TNL-2000T** is the TSOd version. Price: $4,495. The **TNL 2100T** is a Dzus-rail mount version of the TNL-2000T. Price: $8,995.

The **TNL-1000 DC** is a lower-priced version of the TNL-2000. It has the same 6-channel GPS sensor as the upper-end sets. The major differences: the display is LCD, the data card database does not include SUAs, and there is no checklist function. Price: $2,995.

Yet another step-down model is the **TNL 1000** without the DC (for data card) designation. It has an LCD display and a simplified internal database lacking such information as radio frequencies, runways, etc. Price: $2,795.

Note: Trimble's Flightmate handheld is covered in the next chapter.

GARMIN

GARMIN made its debut in 1989 under a previous name: PRONAV. The founders (who, to my knowledge, have not changed *their* names) are Gary Burrell and Min H. Kao, two former Bendix/King executives. Burrell goes back to the early King Radio days of the '60s, and helped design the popular KX 170 nav/comm. More recently, he participated in the development of such products as the KLN 88 loran and the upper-end KLN 670 GPS sensor. Kao also worked on the KLN 670, as well as Bendix/King's loran-based nav management system.

GARMIN pulled off quite a *coup* by being the first manufacturer to be awarded TSO C129, Class A1, enabling their GPS 155 set to be certifiable for IFR nonprecision approaches in addition to enroute and terminal operations. All of the other major players—Trimble, II Morrow, Bendix/King, Northstar, etc.—will eventually offer models that are Class A1 certifiable. However, some of them elected to address the IFR market as quickly as possible with Class A2 sets, which can be certified for enroute and terminal operations, but not approaches. GARMIN went right for the gold, and got it.

The company actually offers three models that are similar enough to be considered a series. The first is the GPS 150, a lower-priced VFR version that operates very much like the 155 but is not TSOd and does not contain the software for IFR approaches. Then there's the GPS

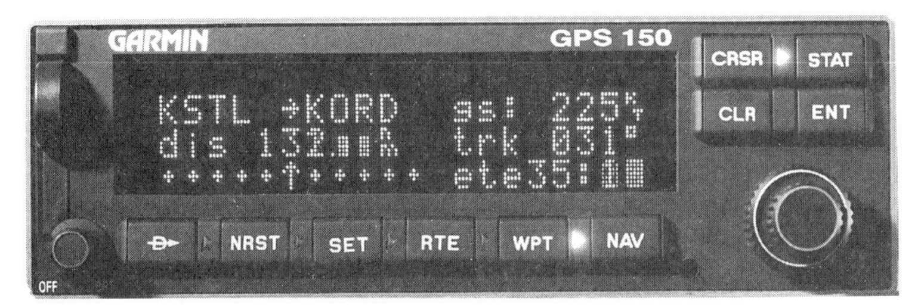

The 150 and 155 are very similar, except that the former is VFR-only and the latter is certifiable for IFR operations.

165, which is a Dzus-rail mount version of the 155, also certified to Class A1.

To simplify matters, I'll describe the **GPS 155** model, and the information will apply to the other two units as well, except as otherwise noted.

How Many Channels? (What, *None?*)

Most manufacturers specify how many channels each of their models has. GARMIN takes a different tack, stating that its system, called MultiTrac,™ is not channelized at all. End of statement, since GARMIN will not go into detail on its proprietary system, lest the competitors latch onto it.

Be that as it may, MultiTrac obviously works well enough to get the FAA's blessing for IFR use.

The set has a 3-line vacuum fluorescent display. It is not as readable as LED in direct sunlight, but GARMIN went to it primarily because of a feature that only they offer at present: a built-in NiCad battery that will provide backup power for up to four hours if the aircraft's electrical system fails. (If the display were LED, which draws much more juice than vacuum fluorescent, the backup battery would provide power for only about seven minutes.)

The set is controlled by two concentric knobs and ten keys. There is a choice of Americas or international database on a user-replaceable data card. The card itself is quite diminutive: only about 1" x 1.5", compared to the approximately 2" x 3.5" card used in many other models.

Included in the database are airports, VORs, NDBs, and intersections. Information includes frequencies; runway IDs, lengths, surface, and lighting; and MSAs. Also, of course, the databases for the 155 and 165 incorporate GPS approaches.

Although comm frequencies for certain types of special use airspace are listed in the airport information pages, there is no SUA alerting function. A "proximity alarm" function allows you to define an alarm circle around a waypoint. This is a nice feature for some purposes (such as avoidance of known obstructions), but a very limited method of devising an SUA alert, especially since you can store only nine proximity waypoints—a drop in the bucket, considering how many SUAs are lurking out there.

The "nearest waypoint" function allows nine waypoints in each category to be called up, along with the two nearest FSS points of communication and frequencies. Nearest airports can be restricted in terms of minimum runway length and type of surface.

One thousand user waypoints can be stored, along with custom comments for all waypoint categories and nine checklists. There is also memory for 20 flight plans of up to 30 legs each.

Among the other functions are a flight simulator mode, VNAV, and E-6B computations.

My Impressions

These impressions are gleaned from using the 150 at home and flying the 165 in GARMIN's Mooney 201.

Operation of the set is straightforward; ten mode keys combine nicely with two knobs for clarity of operation. However, I feel that the keys require an undue amount of pressure to make contact.

What About That Display?

My past experiences with the vacuum fluorescent type of display have left me somewhat in the dark, so to speak, and I regret to say that GARMIN's version also does not shed enough light.

The display is crisp enough indoors or under cloudy skies, but on the bright day of my evaluation flight, I found it difficult to read through my sunglasses. Switching to untinted eyeglasses made the display more readable, but, of course, left me subject to outside glare. Doug Carlson, the factory representative who accompanied me, said that this was a prototype unit and the production models would be brighter. I'll take Doug at his word, but nevertheless, I recommend that anyone who contemplates buying a set with a vacuum fluorescent display should first observe it in direct sunlight.

(Since a GARMIN unit has battery power, you can at least walk it around outside the dealer's shop if you can't get a flight demonstration. Be sure to position the set according to where it will sit in the radio stack.)

Most of my flying time was spent wringing out the approach software. This experience is described in detail in the chapter entitled "Shooting GPS Approaches." For now, suffice it to say that the software does its job and tames even an NDB approach.

To sum up, GARMIN deserves great credit for their no-compromise achievement of energetically obtaining Class A1 certification, especially while some competitors were beating them to the marketplace with Class A2 sets that will later have to be upgraded to Class A1 for approach capability.

In evaluating the receiver as a whole, I have to give it a mixed review. (Again, my comments apply to all three models: the 150, 155, and 165.)

GARMIN's philosophy of providing a battery backup to their panel-mounted units is certainly a worthy enhancement to safety, and will be welcomed especially by instrument pilots, who tend to have a heightened dread of encountering electrical failure while surrounded by gray nothingness. Also, the battery provides a convenient method of programming the set or reviewing its operation in the home, office, or motel without the need for an AC power supply.

But the question arises, is a display that fades somewhat in bright sunlight a reasonable tradeoff for the backup battery? The answer must lie in the eyes of the beholders, some of whom may have no problem whatsoever with the vacuum fluorescent display. (Personally, my vote is for a better type of display; there are other aces in the hole against electrical failure.)

The GPS 150 lists for $2,995. Feature for feature, it stands up very well in relationship to other models in that price class. The GPS 155 is tagged at $4,995, and I feel that the extra two thousand dollars should buy, in addition to IFR capability, SUA alerting and perhaps other features one looks for at that price level. This certainly applies as well to the Dzus-rail mount GPS 165, listing at $5,995.

Note: GARMIN's 95 XL, 55 AVD, and 100 AVD portables are covered in the next chapter.

Bendix/King

Bendix/King, with a long and prestigious pedigree in the nav/comm biz, was tardy in producing a loran, but the unit they finally came up with, the KLN 88, flaunted some sophisticated concepts akin to the high-dollar equipment the manufacturer crafts for the corporate trade—for example, a monochrome CRT (cathode ray tube) display. The KLN 88 has been discontinued, but the concept lives on, in a much-improved GPS series, the latest of which is the **KLN 90B.**

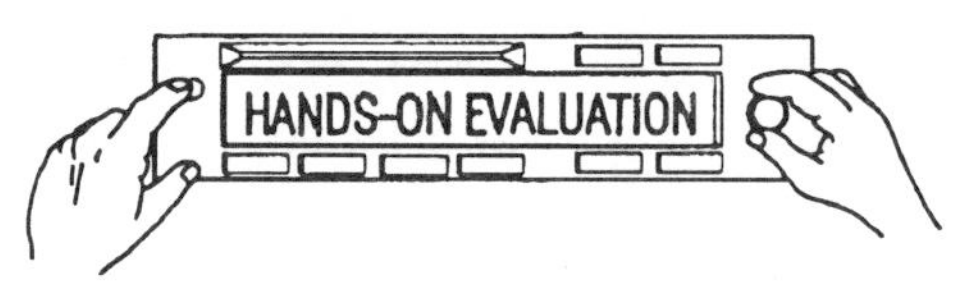

Let me state that my hands-on experience has not been with the KLN 90B; it hasn't even been introduced at this writing, but it is scheduled to come on the market shortly. I had a KLN 88 in my Tiger for several years, and then became acquainted with the KLN 90A. The difference between the 90A and the 90B is that the former is TSOd to C129, Class A2, and the latter is destined for certification to Class A1. (There was also a plain 90, that was not TSOd at all, and thus was strictly VFR.)

Whereas the previous versions had a single-channel GPS sensor, the KLN 90B is equipped with a 6-channel sensor.

Unlike most other sets whose displays are restricted to a certain number of characters occupying two, three, or four lines per page, the KLN 90B's CRT display has virtually unlimited flexibility. You can put lots of information on a given page by using letters and numbers that are small but nevertheless quite legible, thanks to the high resolution of the CRT, plus the fact that you can visually separate categories of information by means of horizontal and vertical lines.

Split Screen Display

The CRT's split screen capability allows you to view two pages of information simultaneously. On the left side of the set is an outer knob, an inner knob, and a button that activates the cursor for the left side of the screen. These controls are duplicated on the right side, although the types of pages for each side are, for the most part, different. The only common page for both sides is the nav page. Another difference: the right inner knob can be pulled out or pushed in for certain additional functions.

In the middle of the set, below the display, are five keys: MSG, for displaying a message the computer has for you (for example, a warning that you are approaching a Class B airspace; ALT, for utilizing the set's altitude alerting function; D, for commanding the set to navigate directly to a waypoint; CLR, for clearing (deleting) an item; and ENT for entering (activating) a command.

Then there's a small knob for turning the set on and adjusting the brightness of the screen.

There are more than 70 individual data pages you can call up and I can't possibly describe them all in just part of a chapter. That would fill a book—and it does! The Pilot's Guide is 8½" x 11" and consists of 137 pages of text and illustrations, all on heavy glossy paper. (In the dark it could easily be mistaken for an issue of *Architectural Digest.*) In the event that this causes you to exceed your plane's weight and balance limitations, you can slip a 5½" x 8 ½" 50-page abbreviated version into your flight bag.

I can hear many of you groaning that you haven't the time to go to night school to learn to operate a GPS receiver. Well, let's face it, the KLN 90B does require a lot of study in order to make use of all its features—because it has so many. But it shouldn't take too much time to learn the basics of going from here to there; then master the more sophisticated functions at your leisure.

Now to some of the KLN 90B's other capabilities

A Large User-Replaceable Database

A Jeppesen NavData database of substantial proportions is encapsulated in a user-replaceable cartridge, which nests in the rear of the set. This is obviously somewhat less convenient than front-loading data cards, but Bendix/King claims that all the KLN 90B's information won't fit on a skinny data card. The database can also be updated by means of a PC.

There's a choice of a North American or international database. Both databases provide worldwide coverage, but the North American database stores more comprehensive information on airports in The US, Canada, and Latin America, while the international database does the same for airports in overseas countries. Also included are airports, VORs, NDBs, and intersections.

Airport information includes city; lat/lon coordinates; elevation; time difference between local time and UTC (Zulu); whether it underlies a Class B or C airspace; type of instrument approach if it has one; runway designation (as well as the runway diagram in many instances), lighting, length, and type of surface for up to five runways; radio frequencies; and a scratchpad page on which you can enter your own memoranda.

In addition, there's right or left traffic pattern direction; availability of services, oxygen, and fuel types; customs; and, most important, whether or not a landing fee is levied (but not how much).

The database can be updated on a one-time basis or by subscription on a quarterly or 28-day cycle. Updates are made by swapping cartridges or via computer disk.

There is storage space for 250 user waypoints, which can be defined by present position, lat/lon, or bearing and distance from an existing waypoint.

Information is the name of the game with the KLN 90B, the idea being to reduce the amount of time you have to spend poring over charts, directories, and the like. For example, when you flip on the power, the set's computer will make a beeline (after some self tests and other clearings of the throat) to a split-screen display that shows, on the right side, an information page for the waypoint that was active when the set was turned off. Chances are that last waypoint was the airport you'd landed at, in which case the right half of the display will be showing you the radio frequencies you will need, such as ATIS, clearance delivery, tower—or, at an uncontrolled field, the CTAF.

And as soon as a GPS position has been acquired, the left side will display your present position in terms of lat/lon and bearing and distance from the nearest high or low frequency VOR. That page keeps updating as you fly, and it's a quick way to verify your current position.

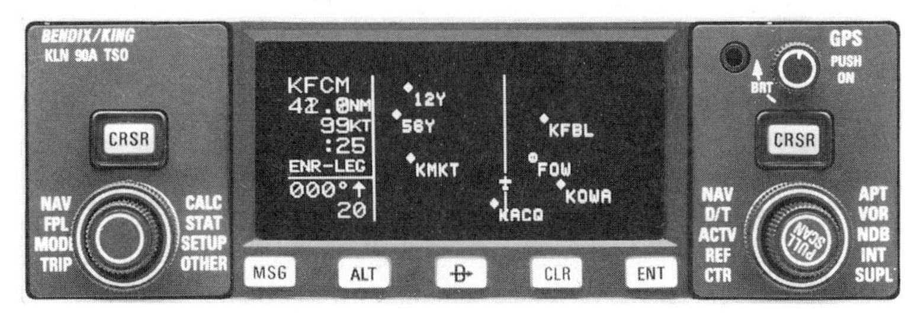

The KLN 90 series features a CRT display and a simple moving map.

FSS and Center Frequencies

The database contains the locations of Flight Service Stations and their remote antenna sites. By dialing up page OTH (for "other") 1, you can display the frequencies for the two nearest FSS facilities, useful for getting weather updates, providing pilot reports, etc.

The OTH 2 page will display the appropriate Center frequencies for the aircraft's position, which is helpful when you want to request VFR flight following. (I wish that Approach frequencies were also included in this feature.)

Sometimes it is desirable to add a waypoint or two along the great circle path of a flight plan, either to see whether the routing will take you through an airport traffic area or other controlled airspace, or to comply with an ATC request for a waypoint within a Center boundary when requesting "RNAV direct." The KLN 90B will compute waypoints that lie on Center boundaries, as well as waypoints defined by radial and distance from selected reference waypoints near the flight path.

Calculator pages will provide E-6B information, such as density altitude, true airspeed, and wind triangles.

Twenty-six flight plans of up to 19 legs each can be stored. A series of trip planning pages enables you to determine the bearing, distance, ETE and fuel required between any two waypoints—not necessarily the ones you are presently using for navigation.

A special use airspace alert page warns you if you are within 10 minutes of penetrating any type of SUA. With altitude input from an encoder, there's an altitude alert function and SUA warnings in 3-D.

A search function calls up the nine nearest airports, VORs, and NDBs. Using the setup function, you can specify the minimum length runway to be included in the airport search, as well as hard-surface runways only. Since the search function can also be used as a quick way of navigating to—or calling up information about—an airport or navaid in the vicinity, I would have preferred to see more than nine in each category; some of the competition offers up to 25!

Super NAV

Now let's get to the meat of any GPS set—the nav pages. By selecting the NAV 1 page with both the left and right outer knobs, you will get what Bendix/King calls a Super NAV 1 page. This includes an ECDI that runs across the entire page, plus digital readouts of the bearing and distance to the waypoint, groundspeed, and ETE. All of this information can also be condensed onto either the left or right half of the screen if you want to view another page at the same time.

MSA and MESA can also be displayed.

Moving Map Display

The NAV 5 page provides a rather simple moving map display. The legs of your flight plan are depicted as a series of lines connecting the waypoints, and a symbol representing your plane moves along the current leg to show where you are on the flight plan. You have a choice of three orientations—north up, desired track up, and actual track up. Also, there is a wide selection of ranges, from 1 to 1000 nm.

By selecting the NAV 5 page on both sides of the screen, you can see symbols representing airports, VORs, and NDBs in their positions relative to the aircraft; each type of symbol can be deselected to reduce clutter. A box on the left side of the screen shows such information as the active waypoint's identifier and distance, and groundspeed and ETE.

Let's look at some more display pages. There is a D/T (distance/time) page that shows the distance and ETE for each waypoint in the active flight plan. Another page will show distances and ETAs in the time zone of your choice. A flight timer can be programmed to start either on power-up or when the aircraft reaches a groundspeed of 30 kn, and the D/T 4 page will display departure time, present time, ETA, flight time, and ETE.

The KLN 90B's data port can be connected to a dedicated version of a Shadin fuel computer. This will enable the set to display the amount of fuel on board, fuel required to reach the destination waypoint (not just the *next* waypoint, as with some other sets), and the amount of fuel you will have on board at the destination. Also, the KLN 90B will interface with Shadin's fuel/air data system, which provides the E-6B information without pilot input.

Good Training

Bendix/King lightens the task of learning the KLN 90B's many features by the high caliber of the Pilot's Guide I referred to earlier. It is written in a conversational tone, is amply illustrated, and is pleasing to the eye. Most important, the Guide actually tells you how to use the set in the real world, which, regrettably, is more than many GPS and loran manuals do. The Guide does have one annoying flaw: its index is woefully inadequate.

There is an optional take-home case that, as its name implies, allows you to play with the set at home, and there is a simulator function that will take you on any trip of your choice. I would ordinarily say that the handsome take-home case, complete with a cooling fan, is a *must*, but I'll downgrade that to a *maybe*, considering the fact that it lists for $702. (Lone Star Aviation's power supply for the KLN 90B doesn't come in a fancy case, but it also has a cooling fan and its price is $249.95.)

My Impression

As I indicated earlier, my comments are based on my experiences with the KLN 88 and KLN 90A. (The difference between the 90A and the 90B is in the latter's nonprecision approach software as well as its certification.) Bendix/King has provided a prodigious number of useful features will appeal to many pilots—but probably not to all, because the more functions a set has, the more strenuous the learning curve. My educational process was aided greatly by working with the sets at home, and by virtually wearing out the Pilot's Guide.

The flight plan mode is well thought out, and easier to edit than some others. This is especially valuable when you're on an IFR flight plan and are given the inevitable amended clearances at the usual inopportune times.

The moving map display is useful, but as I mentioned earlier, it is simple, and that means not as capable as moving maps found in much-lower-priced GPS portables. (But, of course, the set as a whole has many other features found nowhere else.)

Is the KLN 90B for you? Well, if all you need is a no-frills, low-cost GPS receiver, you'd probably view the Bendix/King product as overkill of both your needs and your bank account. But if you have the desire and the dollars for a sophisticated system that can provide you with a host of nav-related information—presented ever so nicely on a CRT display—I think you'll find that the KLN 90B is an outstanding candidate.

The list price was not firmly established at this writing, but it was expected to be approximately $8,500. Also, I've been told that upgrading from a KLN 90 will be no more than $1,750 and upgrading from a KLN 90A will not exceed $975.

Note: Bendix/King's KLX 135, a unit that combines a GPS receiver with a VHF transceiver, is covered in the chapter entitled "A New Breed: GPS/Comms."

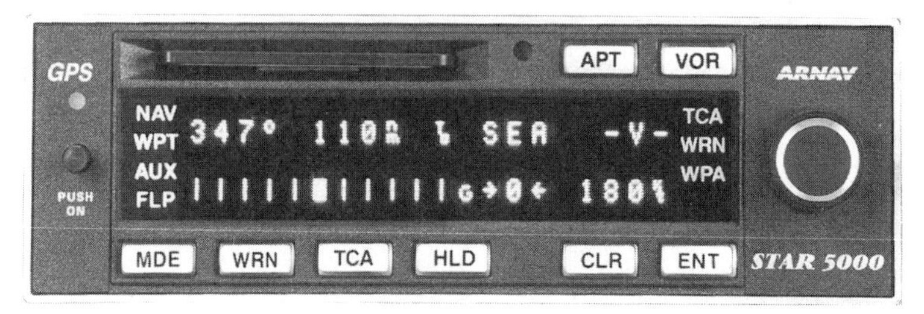

ARNAV offers a choice of loran-only, GPS-only, and multi-sensor systems.

ARNAV

ARNAV was one of the early manufacturers of loran sets for general aviation. The organization evolved from the Morrow Electronics Co. after Ray Morrow lost an internal management war in 1982 and left to form II Morrow. ARNAV has since undergone a couple of ownership changes.

The company's current receiver line includes the FMS 5000 IFR-certifiable loran with GPS option and the Star 5000, a stand-alone GPS unit.

The **FMS 5000** is designed to function as a multi-sensor system and is TSOd to C115a. In its basic form it contains a multi-chain loran sensor that is TSOd to C60b. The set has an LED dot matrix display that will show up to six items at once.

There is a choice of Jeppesen North America, international, and world data card coverages. Waypoint categories include airports, VORs, NDBs, and intersections. Information includes all hard surface public and military airports, frequencies, runway lengths, lighting, and flight rules. Updates are available from Jeppesen every 28 days for an annual charge of $442, or on a one-time basis from ARNAV for $150.

There is storage space for 300 user waypoints that can be defined by radial and distance from an existing waypoint as well as by present position and lat/lon.

The set has an alert function for all types of special use airspace, including three-dimensional alerts for Class B, C, and D airspace. There is also an altitude deviation warning.

You can create any number of flight plans to a maximum of 100 waypoints. A search function calls up the 15 nearest airports, VORs, and intersections.

Remote ranging shows the bearing and distance between any two waypoints. Other functions include minimum safe altitude, VNAV, and winds aloft computations.

For training at home, a simulated flight mode has a default route from Pendleton, Oregon (PDT) to Seattle International (SEA); or you can plug in your favorite route.

In its loran-only configuration, the FMS 5000 lists for $4,495. With an optional GPS sensor, the FMS 5000 is TSOd to C115a and will automatically select GPS or loran, whichever is providing the better position information. Actually, you have a choice of two GPS sensors. For general aviation use, ARNAV recommends the 5-channel GPS-505 sensor, packaged with the FMS 5000 for $6,995. The 12-channel GPS-512 is offered for differential GPS operations that can circumvent the Selective Availability degradation. Its price with the FMS 5000 is $8,995.

The **Star 5000** is a GPS-only receiver with a 5-channel sensor. It has most of the operational features of the FMS 5000. Price: $4,495. It will be upgradable to C129 at a cost of $750. The **FMS 7000** is a Dzus-rail mount version of the 5000. Price: $9,995 with your choice of loran or a 5-channel GPS sensor; $10,995 with both; and $12,995 with the loran and 12-channel GPS sensor.

ARNAV also manufactures the MFD 5000 multi-function display, which is described in the chapter entitled "Other Types of Moving Map Systems."

Northstar

Northstar Technologies is now a division of Canadian Marconi, a leading manufacturer of corporate and commercial equipment. The venerable M1 loran has been phased out of production and the current

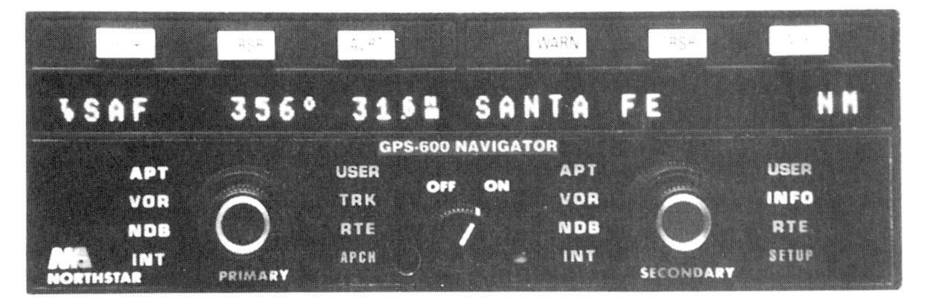

Northstar sets feature a split-screen LED display with many combinations of pages

line consists of the M2 loran (available as a multi-sensor system with a GPS sensor); the M3, GPS-600, and GPS-60 stand-alone GPS receivers; and the C1, a very interesting new VHF comm add-on to the aforementioned models.

The M3 is not, as its designation suggests, a later iteration of the M1 and M2 lorans. Rather, it is a TSOd version of the GPS-600, certifiable under C129, Class A2. (At this writing, Northstar plans to seek Class A1 sometime in the future.) All of the Northstar models operate in pretty much the same way, so the following description of the M3 applies generally (but not entirely) to the other sets; I'll explain the differences at appropriate places.

The **M3** is a 12-channel GPS receiver with Northstar's traditional dual LED dot matrix display that allows you a considerable amount of flexibility in determining what types of data you want to have exhibited at any given time. For example, while monitoring the bearing and distance to your next waypoint on the left side, you can call up the bearing and distance to another airport, VOR, NDB, or intersection on the right side. Or you might choose to activate the "nearest airport" function on the second side; it will automatically update, always showing bearing and distance to the airport that is closest to your present position.

There are many other options. For example, you can call up a single page, running the entire width of the display, that shows ETE, groundspeed, and bearing and distance to the next waypoint.

Buttons and Knobs

There are two pairs of knobs that are used to scroll through the database, enter input, and call up information. In addition, there is a row of six buttons at the top of the set. Pressing the D (direct) button instantly defines a flight path from your present position to the waypoint or flight plan leg displayed in the primary readout.

Two CRSR buttons activate the cursors for the primary and secondary displays respectively. An ALRT button lights up to caution you that you are near a chunk of special use airspace. A red WARN button flashes to alert you that the GPS signals are unreliable; press the button and a displayed message will describe the situation. You can also press WARN at any time to display the set's estimation of its current accuracy.

The Database

The database comes on a user-replaceable data card and covers all of the US, Canada, Mexico, Central America, and parts of northern Colombia and Venezuela. In addition, there are 178 airports of entry worldwide. Included are airports, VORs, NDBs, and intersections, as well as Class B and C airspace, prohibited, restricted, and warning areas, and MOAs. There is memory for 250 user waypoints, which can be defined by present position, lat/lon, or bearing and distance from an existing waypoint. Here's something new and interesting: the database contains all published US and Canadian victor airways and jet routes.

Airport information includes city and state; frequencies; field elevation; runway designation, length, and type of surface for up to five runways; type of instrument approach (precision, nonprecision or none); whether lighted; and latitude and longitude.

The search function includes the 20 nearest airports, VORs, NDBs, and intersection. In addition, the set will display the nearest victor airways and jet routes.

Getting There

In addition to navigating direct from your present position to any waypoint, you can enter a track—say, 270 degrees from your present position—and the M3 will provide steering information that will keep you on that track, VOR style. There is also a parallel track function, with the offset adjustable from 1 to 20 nm to the left or right of course.

Another display provides plain English deviation information, for example, "FLY RIGHT 1.2 NM." If you deviate from your programmed flight path by more than 4 nm, you will get an "OFF-COURSE ALARM" message.

The M3 can store 20 flight plans of up to 98 legs each. There is a turn command function.

A warning message appears when you program a flight path that will cause you to penetrate a controlled area.

The alert function can be disabled for a single controlled area, or for all areas. When the function is disabled, you will receive a reminder message to that effect each time you power up the set.

Other Functions

To activate the ETA function, you set the M3's clock in accordance with any one of a menu of 19 time zones. You can then access any other time zone and the ETA display will adjust accordingly.

The winds aloft function combines the set's computation of current track and groundspeed with the pilot's input of heading and TAS.

A Demo/Look-Ahead feature is divided into two modes. The Demo mode is designed for demonstrating the features of the set or for user training on the ground. Demo allows you to enter any two waypoints, plus a course and groundspeed, for a simulated trip. The M3 will then fly the trip, displaying all navigation features including crosstrack error, ETE, nearest airports, SUA airspace alerts, etc. Demo will operate only if the set is disconnected from the aircraft antenna, in order to preclude its inadvertent use in flight.

The Look-Ahead mode can be accessed when the set is installed in the aircraft. As its name implies, it allows you to look ahead to any waypoint in the database. You can use this function to call up information pertaining to the 20 nearest airports at your destination, as an aid in selecting suitable alternates.

Price: $6,395.

The **GPS-600** is similar to the M3, except that it has a 6-channel sensor versus the M3's 12-channel sensor; also, it is not TSOd and therefore is VFR-only. Price: $4,995. The GPS-600 can be upgraded to an M3 for $1,000.

The **GPS-60** is a budget version of the GPS-600. Its standard database does not have the Victor airways, Jet routes, and private airstrips. However, the full database of the more expensive units is available for $175 extra, which makes the set equivalent to a GPS-600, except that it cannot be upgraded to IFR certifiability. Price: $3,495.

The **M2** is the loran version of the GPS-600. It has a single-chain sensor and is certifiable to C60b for IFR enroute and terminal operations. With the addition of a remote-mounted GPS sensor, you have a multi-sensor system certifiable to C115a, at a total price of $6,992.50.

The **SmartComm** is a remote-mounted VHF transceiver that utilizes the controls, display, and position information of a Northstar GPS or loran receiver (any model except the M1) to offer easy access to the frequencies of facilities in the aircraft's vicinity. For further details, see the chapter entitled "A New Breed: GPS/Comms."

Magellan

Magellan Systems has been manufacturing GPS receivers for the marine world since 1989. Shortly thereafter, the company looked at the aviation market, went as far as to offer its GPS sensor to other OEMs (original equipment manufacturers), then decided to come out with its own aviation line.

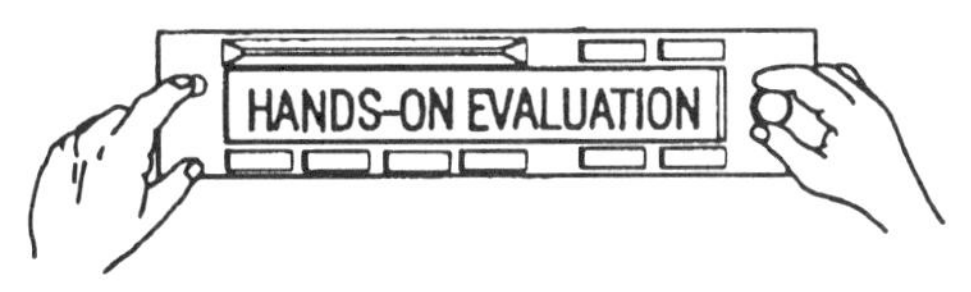

The **SkyNav 5000** is a 5-channel GPS set with a vacuum fluorescent display. It is not TSOd at this writing, but Magellan plans to seek Class A2 and possibly A1.

The set's database comes on a data card with coverage of either North, Central, and South America or the rest of the world. Included are airports, VORs, NDBs, intersections, and DMEs (in Europe, DMEs are stand-alone navaids). Information includes comm frequencies, runway data, and something not often provided and very nice to have—ILS identifiers and frequencies.

There is storage for 1,000 user waypoints, which can be defined by present position, lat/lon, or bearing and distance from an existing waypoint. Custom comments of up to 34 characters each can be appended to as many as 500 waypoints in any database category. A comment can also be programmed to display itself shortly after power-up. This could be a reminder such as ANNUAL DUE IN JUNE. You have to acknowledge the comment by pressing the ENTER key, at which point the set automatically goes into the nav mode.

There is memory for 20 flight plans of up to 20 legs apiece. The course and distance for each leg of a selected flight plan can be displayed, and a summary page shows the total distance of the route.

There are five nav pages, as follows: Page 1—ID, bearing, and distance to next waypoint; track; groundspeed; CDI. Page 2—IDs of FROM and TO waypoints; track; crosstrack error shown digitally; groundspeed. Page 3—Present position in lat/lon. Page 4—Altitude. Page 5—ETA (in the time zone of your choice); ETE; current time.

The nearest waypoint function points the way to the five closest waypoints in each category.

Magellan's SkyNav 5000 can be programmed to remind you when your plane's annual is due—or your BFR, medical, etc..

The AUX mode enables you to select a number of parameters, including the satellite mask angle and 2D versus 3D, if you should want to make those choices (not really necessary under normal conditions of satellite coverage). Speaking of 2D, Magellan offers a compatible blind encoder for the automatic entry of altitude with 2D reception ($495) and a converter for your existing encoder ($395).

Countdown and countup timer functions are activated in the AUX mode. For you data port freaks, the SkyNav 5000 comes with *two.*

My Impressions

The set is easy to use, following the obligatory pre-flight familiarization with the user manual. (And congratulations, Magellan, your user manual is well written and well organized.) The key-and-knob combinations for accessing or inputting data are straightforward and logical. In some respects, the 5000 behaves like a higher-priced model.

I have a small quarrel with what I would call the basic nav page—the one displaying the most desirable information. That seems to be the 5000's first nav page, and I would prefer it to show ETE instead of track.

More important, the 5000 does not have an SUA alert. This is an unfortunate omission, considering the constant proliferation of chunks of sky that require negotiations with air traffic control. Since GPS can take you direct at the press of a button, it's very helpful to be reminded when you need to go somewhat *indirect.* I hope Magellan adds SUAs to the database in the future.

Now let's view that vacuum fluorescent display—at least, as seen in the Mooney that I was using. The news is mixed. In conditions other than direct sunlight, the display was a lot more legible and more pleasant to look at than an LCD. In fact, it was comparable to the more expensive LED readouts. But when the sun beamed in, the vacuum fluorescent display washed out and my hand became a portable glareshield. (The overall legibility might vary somewhat, depending on the aircraft and the set's location in the panel. For more on this subject, see the section on GARMIN's models.)

In sum, the SkyNav 5000 is a capable performer with sensible architecture and a lot of good features. It doesn't offer every amenity that the higher-priced models have, but it certainly is a strong contender in its price range.

Price: $2,675. Note: Magellan's MAP 7000 handheld is covered in the next chapter.

Narco

Narco's bread and butter traditionally has been in VHF nav/comms and DMEs. Now the company is combining that background with GPS technology to offer a flight management system related in concept to some of the corporate-type black boxes—yet it's panel-mounted and priced for the general aviation market.

The **Star*Nav NS 9000** is a multi-sensor unit that combines an internal 5-channel GPS sensor with VOR and glideslope receivers. The system can also interface with a compatible DME and any loran receiver that has an RS-232 data port. Once the system is initialized, its computer searches a built-in database for the 10 nearest VOR and

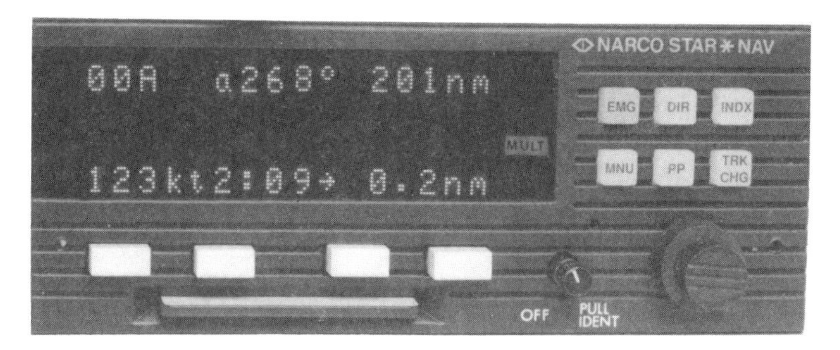

The NS 9000 can blend GPS with VOR, DME, and loran signals.

DME stations and chooses the stations that can offer the best accuracy. Data is blended in from GPS and (if installed) loran, using a weighting system based on the expected accuracy of each position fix. The computer then calculates the aircraft's position, which Narco states will be more accurate than any one of the individual fixes.

The set has a dot matrix LED display; controls consist of ten keys. There is memory for 99 user waypoints, which can be defined by lat/lon or present position, but not by radial and distance from an existing waypoint. A Jeppesen database, supplied on a user-updatable data card, covers North America and contains airports, VORs, NDBs, and intersections. Airport data includes field elevation; radio frequencies; runway length, surface, and lighting; and availability of instrument approach.

A search function calls up the 10 nearest airports and VORs. Five flight plans of 10 legs each can be stored. The frequencies of ATC and FSS facilities appropriate to the aircraft's position can be displayed. Other features include minimum safe altitude and special use airspace alert for all SUAs.

Dimensions: 2.5" H x 6.25" W x 11" D. Price: $5,539. A GPS-only version, the **GPS 900**, lists for $3,595.

Ashtech

Ashtech has produced GPS receivers for a variety of commercial applications since its founding in 1987. The company was the first to market a commercial 12-channel receiver. Now Ashtech has entered the world of aviation.

The **Altair AV-12** has a 12-channel GPS sensor and features a three-color CRT display with moving map capability. Its database comes on a data card with a choice of North America or international

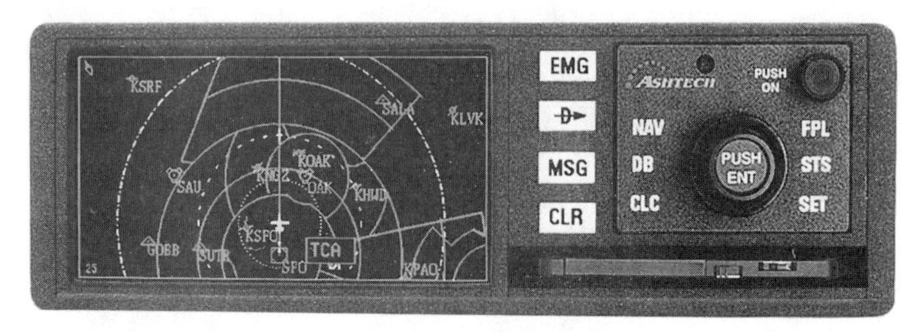

Ashtech's Altair AV-1 boasts a color CRT display, a full-featured moving map, and a 12-channel GPS sensor.

coverage. Included are airports, VORs, NDBs, and intersections, as well as special use airspace. Information includes frequencies, runway diagrams, lighting, fuel, and Morse code identifiers of VORs and NDBs.

There is storage for 1000 user waypoints and 100 flight plans with any number of legs up to 1000 waypoints.

Flight plans can be programmed on a PC and then transferred to the AV-12 via a card reader.

The moving map display has split-screen capability for showing the map on the left side and navigation or other information on the right side. There is no approach mode; Ashtech believes that the map should not be used as a reference for approaches because of safety considerations.

Ashtech plans to apply for TSO C129, Class A2 initially. The system is priced at $8,500.

Terra

Terra started out as a manufacturer of small panel-mounted nav/comms and handhelds, and has diversified by acquiring a line of radar altimeters and airborne telephones. The **TGPS 400 D** is actually Trimble's TNL-1000 DC with Terra's nameplate on it. The list price is also the same as Trimble's—$2,995—but Terra offers special package prices for the GPS receiver in combination with its comm transceivers.

Ross Engineering

The **LCA 200** loran can now be converted to a multi-sensor system with the addition of a GPS sensor and antenna. The unit has a segmented LCD display and a keypad. There is storage for 200 user waypoints and 20 flight plans of up to 25 legs each.

According to the manufacturer, the system's computer uses a custom position-solution program that measures the distance, stability, and gradient of the loran signals and then calculates the aircraft's position by blending all of the usable signal information it receives. There is no factory database.

Base price of the LCA 200 is $995. The GPS kit, including an external antenna, costs an additional $1,394.95; an antenna for use on the glareshield may be offered in the future. A mounting tray is available for $119.95. For loran reception, the set can be connected to the aircraft's by means of a coupler that is provided. Dimensions: 3" H x 6.25" W x 7.5" D.

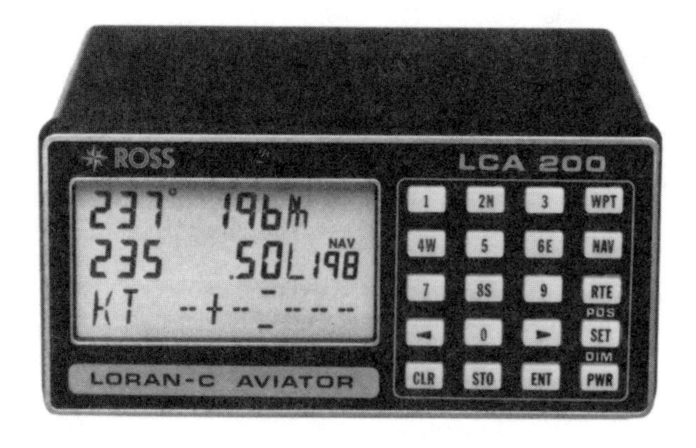

According to Ross, their LCA 200 can utilize the aircraft's comm antenna by means of a coupler.

10

GPS Handhelds

GPS handheld receivers have generated a lot of interest—for good reason. For one thing, they offer GPS nav capability at very reasonable prices, which become even more reasonable when you consider that they will operate right out of the box without installation cost.

Being portable, they can provide multiple service in more than one aircraft—which is great for renters—and they can also be used in a boat, land vehicle, or on the hiking trail.

They will serve as backup navigation in the event of an aircraft electrical system failure, and could guide you on a trek to civilization if you had a forced landing in a desolate area.

Avionics shop managers tell me that customers who have loran or other area nav installations are acquiring GPS handhelds as an inexpensive way to utilize satellite navigation while waiting for GPS to achieve full IFR status in the national airspace system.

Although handhelds tend not to have as many features as their panel-mounted counterparts, there is one notable exception: several handheld models now incorporate moving map displays, a feature not found on most panel-mounted GPS receivers.

You may wonder how good a moving map display can be in a handheld. In my view it's quite good; as far as display size is concerned, both the Apollo 920 and the GARMIN 95 XL windows measure approximately 2.25" W by 1.5" H, which would be roughly comparable to the display of Eventide's panel-mounted Argus 5000 if the latter were turned on its side. Sony's IPS-760 handheld has an even larger display. (Size, of course, is not the only consideration. For example, the Eventide units have a CRT display versus the plainer LCD of the handhelds, plus some unique options, but the handheld moving maps are quite sophisticated in their own right; more on that later.)

As with panel-mounted receivers, each handheld model is different from all the rest, and I'll provide the major features and specifications of every unit currently available. Before doing that, however, let's look at some general considerations.

Antennas. Since GPS signals are line-of-sight, the only satellites you can receive at any given time are those that are in view of the antenna; the signals cannot pass through any metallic portions of the aircraft. Thus, antennas that are used inside the aircraft are either affixed to the windshield (usually with a suction cup) or placed atop the glareshield, in order to "see" as many satellites as possible. Some handhelds have a single detachable antenna, while others have an internal antenna and a second remote antenna.

By and large, these inside-mounted antennas perform quite well, although they detract somewhat from the neatness of the cockpit. Those users who demand a cleaner and more secure installation, along with optimum signal acquisition, can install an external antenna at a cost of about $400 plus labor.

Power. Most units are powered by either four or six AA alkaline batteries, with accessories (standard or optional, depending on the manufacturer) that may include a NiCad pack and AC charger, a cigarette lighter adapter, and/or cabling that can be connected to the avionics bus. Be aware that if the set is hard-wired to the aircraft's electrical system (or to an external antenna), the system may lose its portable status and require a field approval.

Controls. All of the handhelds are operated strictly by pushbuttons. Some have full alphanumeric keypads while others are controlled by just a few multi-function keys. It may appear that the former would be more straightforward than the latter, but in my view this is not necessarily the case. Ease of use is more a function of the operating software than anything else. I should add that any one of the sets will demand home study time—in some cases, with not much help from the user manual. Now here are the GPS handheld models, listed by manufacturer.

II Morrow

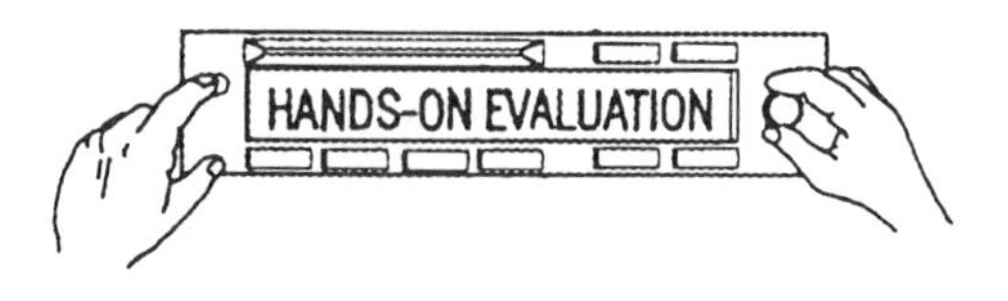

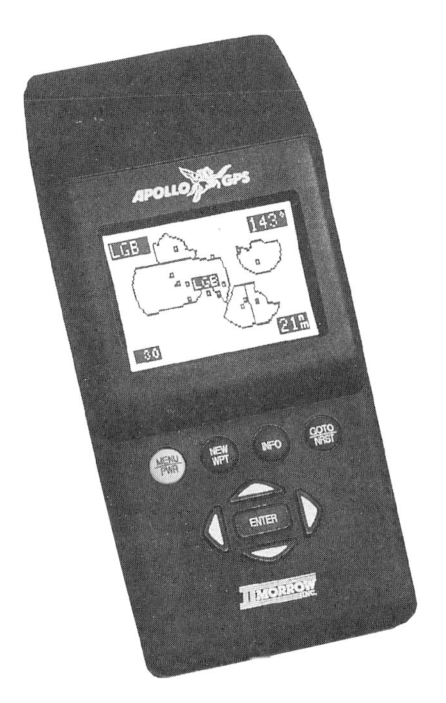

II Morrow's Apollo 920 has Auto Zoom and a host of other nice features.

The **Apollo 920** has a rugged look and feel, due in no small part to the rubber-like material that covers the top half of the unit. (The set is water-resistant, presumably for mariners as well as for amphibious pilots who might absent-mindedly lower the gear for a water landing.) Dimensions are 3.7" W x 7.8" H x 2" D and the weight is 1.45 lb with six AA batteries in place. The batteries provide juice for approximately six hours; a power cable with cigarette lighter plug is also included.

The set has a built-in antenna for general use and a remote aircraft antenna in the form of a 2 ⅛" diameter disc that can be suction-cupped to the windshield or simply laid atop the glareshield.

The 920's display is LCD and its usable area measures approximately 2.25" W x 1.5" H. That sounds small for a moving map display, but it is actually quite adequate if the set is positioned in the pilot's immediate view, and for this purpose II Morrow provides a yoke mounting bracket.

The GPS sensor has six channels and can track up to six satellites simultaneously.

The purchaser can choose one of three internal databases. The first one covers North America, Central America, and the Caribbean; the second one covers the US—except for Hawaii and Alaska—along with South America and Mexico; the third one covers the rest of the world.

PC Updatable

The databases can be updated by means of an optional ($29.95) cable that connects to a PC. Updates are provided on disk at a cost of $100 for a single update and $249 for four.

Standard equipment includes one database, the yoke mount, cigarette lighter power cable, a second power cable for hard wiring, the external antenna, and a carrying case.

The database categories include airports, VORs, NDBs, and enroute intersections. There is memory for 2000 user waypoints, that can be defined by present position or lat/lon, but not by bearing and distance from an existing waypoint.

The information that's provided by the database is comparable to that found on many panel-mounted units. The data on each airport includes the identifier; city; state; country; facility name; lat/lon; field elevation; comm frequencies; runway designation, length, surface; lighting; and a runway diagram.

The set is controlled by function keys labeled MENU/PWR, NEW WPT, INFO, and GO TO/NRST—along with four arrow keys for entering data and making selections, and an ENTER key.

The MENU/PWR key brings the unit to life and can be used to turn the backlighting on at low or high intensity. When you power up the unit, you see the first page of the nav mode, consisting of a bar graph display of the signal strength of the satellites in view. Pressing the up or down arrow key gets you the following nav pages: altitude, lat/lon, and an ECDI (electronic course deviation indicator); range, bearing, desired track, time, actual track, and ECDI; range, bearing, groundspeed, ETE (estimated time enroute), track, and ECDI; a moving map display with a box on the right side containing numeric nav information; a moving map display without the nav info box; and a route plan list.

Press the MENU/PWR key again and you get to a main menu offering a choice of setups and other options. For example, you can enter the operation mode and change from inflight navigation to a simulator function. There you can program a simulated flight between the waypoints of your choice—including a multi-waypoint route plan—enter a groundspeed, and the 920 will proceed to fly that route, complete with nav displays, airspace alerts, etc. This is an excellent way of learning the many functions of the unit and doing your flight planning in the comfort of your home, motel, or wherever you happen to be.

Other Ways to Go

The operation mode also offers marine, survey, land mobile, and hiking selections. The differences are not significant, except that the marine mode provides an orthographic screen, which is a type of ECDI favored by some skippers.

The moving map display shows all categories of waypoints: airports, VORs, NDBs, intersections, user, and (in the future) cities. It also depicts the outlines of all types of special use airspace, but not the altitude segments. A track history can be displayed, in the form of dotted lines showing the straight-arrow or embarrassingly erratic path your flight has taken. Any of the aforementioned items can be deleted from the screen to reduce clutter.

You have a choice of map orientations: track up, desired track up, and north up.

There are 15 range settings, from 0.1 to 750 nm. In cruise, I normally choose a setting in the 20-40 nm range, switching to a lower setting as I approach my destination. The 920 has a very handy setting called Auto Zoom, which automatically maintains whatever range is necessary to keep the destination waypoint in view. The way I recommend using this is to switch from whatever fixed range setting you're utilizing to AUTO when you get fairly close to your destination. As you approach the airport, the range setting will continually decrease, providing you with more detail. This includes a runway diagram, which zooms larger and larger as you get closer and closer.

To obtain information on any waypoint shown on the moving map, press the ENTER key until that waypoint is highlighted, then press the INFO key. You can also get information pages by manually entering the desired waypoint's identifier.

Airport information includes the identifier; bearing and distance from present position; city; state; country; facility name; lat/lon; field elevation; comm frequencies; type of fuel available; landing fee; IFR capability; runway designation, length, surface; lighting; and runway diagram.

Press the GO TO/NRST and you'll get a page showing bearing, distance, and other info on the nearest waypoint in the category you have last selected (not necessarily the nearest airport). Press the key again and you'll see a list of the 30 nearest waypoints, regardless of category. I'm not too fond of this method, preferring to see nearest airports first; if I need to land in a hurry, I'd invariably rather set down on an airport than a VOR station.

There is memory for 20 routes of up to 29 legs apiece.

A waypoint arrival message can be programmed to come on at your choice of distances up to nine nm. If the waypoint is within a route plan, the heading to your next waypoint will be displayed. There is also a message that's programmable by distance and time, warning you that you are approaching some type of special use airspace.

Other features include parallel track and a countdown timer.

My Impressions

This is a really super unit! The displays are easy to read, and the information is well organized and quite complete for a handheld model. I really like the choice of map displays, the Auto Zoom feature, and the many ways in which the set can be customized.

Also, I've been pleasantly surprised to find that, while other handhelds I've tried seem to suck the life out of alkaline batteries like Dracula with a tapeworm, the 920 keeps going...and going...and... (Has II Morrow discovered the secret of eternal battery life?)

Anything I don't like? Well, he-e-ere we go again: the user manual. (Sigh.) Actually, II Morrow calls it a User's Guide, and this Guide is a Gnome. It measures about 3⅛" W by 4¼" H and the idea was to make it teeny weeny so it would fit in the pocket of the 920's carrying case. Never mind that it leaves you to puzzle out the most effective ways to use some of the functions, such as the simulator and Auto Zoom. A better approach would have been to provide a manual of the size necessary to properly educate the user and slip a slender quick reference guide in the pocket.

The good news about all of this is that the 920's architecture is so straightforward that you'll be able to use most of the functions intuitively—but I do wish that II Morrow, once and for all, would decide to make their instructional material as complete and imaginative as most of their current black boxes. Even if it involves some manual labor. (Sorry.)

That caveat to one side, the 920 is an excellent entry in the GPS handheld derby. I found it a joy to use. Price: $1,595.

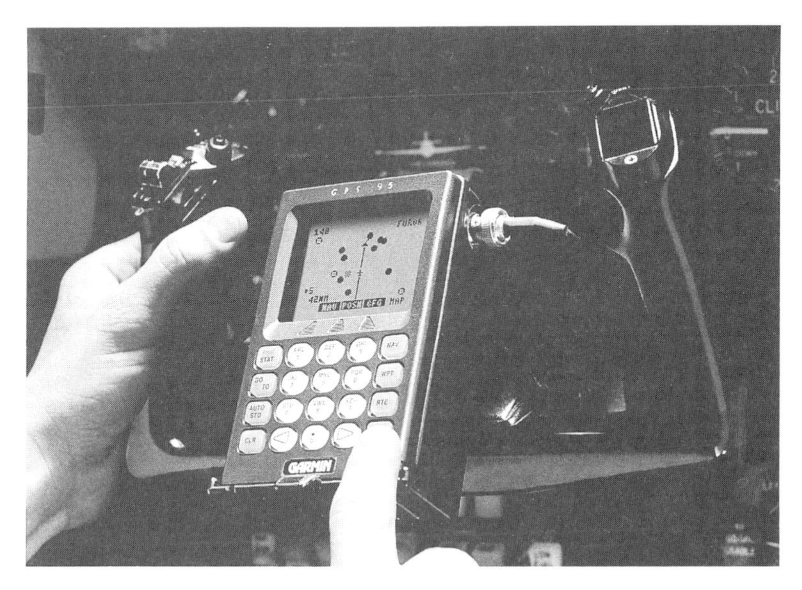

GARMIN has provided the 95 XL with Auto Zoom and detailed depictions of special use airspace.

GARMIN

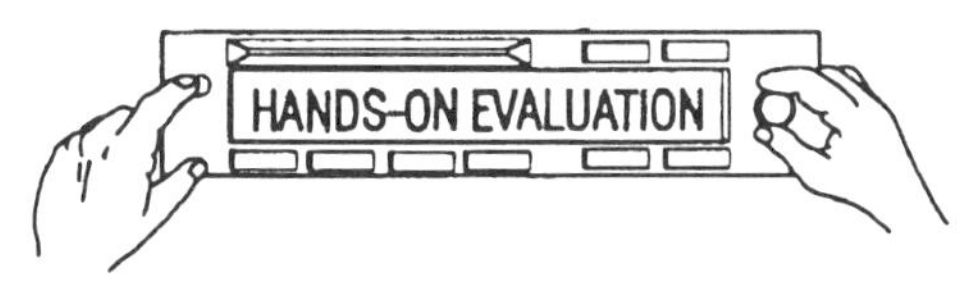

The **95 XL** is an improved version of the model that preceded it, the 95 AVD. It comes in a package that's 4.9" H x 3.2" W x 1.5" D, including a removable battery pack. The set's single-channel sensor can track up to eight satellites simultaneously.

Juice is provided several ways: by four AA alkaline batteries; by an optional NiCad pack; or by a cigarette lighter power cord. Of course, you can also wire it directly into your aircraft's electrical system.

The antenna is attached to the unit by means of a BNC connector. A cable-and-suction-cup accessory is provided for mounting the antenna to the aircraft's windshield.

Other standard accessories include a AA battery pack, cigarette lighter adapter, power/data cable, and yoke mount.

The unit has an internal database with a choice of either the Americas or international coverage. Waypoints comprise airports, VORs, NDBs, and intersections. Included in the airports section are: the identifier; city; state; country; facility name; lat/lon; field elevation; comm frequencies; runway designation, length, surface; lighting; and a graphic depiction of runway configuration.

The database can be updated by means of a personal computer interface. The cable costs $30, and updates on disk are priced at $100 for a one-time update, $250 for a quarterly subscription, and $675 for an annual subscription with revisions every 28 days.

The set has memory for 500 user waypoints, which can be defined by present position, lat/lon, or bearing and distance from an existing waypoint. (For some reason, the user manual does not include the "present position" method in the section titled "Creating User Waypoints." Instead, the persevering reader will eventually find it in a section all its own, under the pretentious title Autostore™—as if every other manufacturer did not offer this basic function.)

A brief custom comment (20 characters) can be entered for each user waypoint.

The unit is controlled by a keypad consisting of 20 buttons, three of which are "soft" keys whose functions vary according to the mode in use.

A lot of the information is accessed by highlighting a data field by means of two cursor arrows, and then changing the field if necessary by pressing the CLR key. For example, the Navigation Summary page might show your bearing, distance, track, and groundspeed to the waypoint, along with an ECDI. If you want to substitute ETE or ETA for groundspeed, you use an arrow key to highlight "GS" and press CLR until ETE or ETA shows up. There are other options as well, allowing you to customize the page according to your preferences.

A Present Position page shows your track, groundspeed, lat/lon, and time of day.

SUAs Now on the Map

Last, but certainly not least, the star of our show, the Map Display. It depicts up to 15 of the nearest waypoints in each category (airports, VORs, etc.), depending on the scale selected, along with a plot of your track. The predecessor model, the GPS 95 AVD, did not depict special use airspace, but the 95 XL shows sectorized Class B and C, as well as all other types of SUA; older sets can be upgraded for $250.

There are 10 range settings, allowing you to zoom in as close as a half mile or extend out to as distant as 240 nm. At the lower range settings you will see runway diagrams for certain airports—apparently the Federally designated ones with alphabetical identifiers.

GARMIN has added the Auto Zoom feature that I found so useful in the Apollo 920.

To obtain information on any waypoint shown on the map, move the cursor onto the desired waypoint and press the ENT key. Then if you want to navigate to that waypoint, press the GO TO key and that waypoint will immediately become your new destination.

To reduce clutter, you can deselect any category of waypoints. There's a choice of map orientations: north up, ground track up, or heading up.

Basic Point-A-to-Point-B navigation to a destination that's not on the map is fairly easy. Use the aforementioned GO TO key and punch in the identifier of the desired waypoint. Airports, VORs, and NDBs can also be accessed by entering either the facility name or the city in which it is located.

Entering alphanumerics by means of a multifunction keypad is not exactly zippy, but you get used to it.

Good Flight Planning

Twenty flight plans of up to 29 legs each can be stored. When checking out the flight plan architecture of a unit, I pay close attention to how easily a route can be created and, especially, edited. You can build routes at your leisure at home, but if something like a pop-up thunderstorm causes you to change your plans in flight, you want to be able to massage that route without delving into the manual. The 95 XL has a good, straightforward route management system.

A search function will provide information on the nine nearest waypoints in each category. Unfortunately, the 95 XL does not have a dedicated method of automatically directing you to the nearest *airport,* which is what you want in an emergency. For example, if the last waypoint category you had been using was VORs, activating the "nearest" function would give you a list of the nine closest VORs and you'd have to go through a separate process to change to the airport category, which is what you really want if the engine is sputtering. (This is the same complaint I made of the Apollo 920.)

You can select a minimum runway length and type of surface for the airport search, in case you're flying a homebuilt bizjet.

The set has a simulator mode that allows you to program the flight of your choosing, including a route plan, and utilize the 95 XL's many functions as you go.

Other features include VNAV and such E-6B computations as density altitude, true airspeed, winds aloft, and fuel planning. Price: $1,495.

The **55 AVD** handheld lacks the moving map feature, has a less comprehensive database, and is saddled with the old-fashioned and unattractive segmented display. With its list price of $1,295, not that far below much more sophisticated models, I can think of no reason to choose it.

The **100 AVD** is a portable of panel-size dimensions: 2" H x 6.25" W x 3.95" D. It was actually designed to be used either as a portable unit or, with a mounting tray and external fixed antenna, as a panel-mounted set. The 100 AVD has an LCD display and a built-in NiCad battery that can be trickle-charged by the aircraft's electrical system when installed in the panel, or recharged by a 110V AC charger.

The database is internal and is available in a choice of North American, international, and worldwide coverages. Included are airports, VORs, NDBs, and intersections. Airport information includes the field elevation, lat/lon, and bearing and distance from the nearest VOR. The waypoints are not listed by name, only by identifier. There is memory for 100 user waypoints and 10 flight plans of up to nine legs each. Price: $2,495.

Trimble

The **Flightmate Pro** has replaced the original Flightmate GPS handheld, which was handicapped by complex connections to its accessories that resulted in an annoying and unsightly jumble of wires. By contrast, the Pro is lean cuisine with much less spaghetti. In addition, the software has been enhanced, and a serial data port has been added.

The unit has internal and external antennas. Power is supplied by four AA batteries or a battery eliminator pack and cigarette lighter cable, which are standard equipment. A yoke mount is also standard.

The set is sleek, slim, and attractive; its dimensions are 6.8" H x 3.3" W x 1.3" D.

A 3-channel sensor tracks up to eight satellites. The set has a four-line LCD display and eight rubber control keys, whose functions are indicated by pictographs—no words at all. This suggests that you should be able to work the thing without too much difficulty, and that proves to be the case. Press the power key and the display enlightens you with a few pages of basic instructions, which you can skip by pressing the return key. There are plain English prompts on other display pages as well. Of course, you will want to read the manual.

The Flightmate has seven operating modes: NAV, WPT, NEAR, TRIP, TIME, MORE, and GPS. You get into the mode you want by pressing a left or right arrow key.

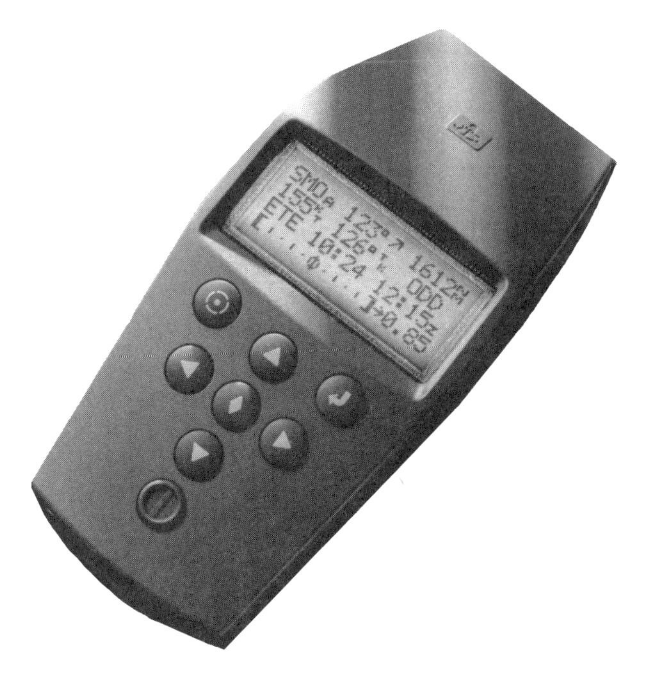

Trimble's Flightmate Pro is not the fanciest of the GPS handhelds, but the price is right.

Since you might want to set up some waypoints before you go flying, let's start with the WPT mode. The worldwide database airports, VORs, and NDBs.

The only information displayed for airports is the identifier, lat/lon, and field elevation. For VORs and NDBs, the identifier, lat/lon, and frequency are shown. Updates are available at the factory for $125 each.

There is memory for 100 user waypoints, which can be defined by present position, lat/lon, or radial and distance from an existing waypoint. Names can be assigned to the user waypoints. Ten flight plans of up to 10 legs each can be stored.

A "copy waypoint" function allows you to duplicate airports and VORs as user waypoints; this enables you to organize them more readily for flight planning.

Walk Before You Fly

The manual suggests that you start the learning process by taking the Flightmate for a walk. This is not a bad idea, since if you become fixated on the operation of the unit, it's better to hit a mailbox at 2 knots than a mountain at 120.

During your stroll, you can find out how many satellites you are acquiring and the signal strength of each by inquiring in the GPS and MORE modes. It is in the GPS mode that you enter your altitude manually if you are receiving only three satellites.

The NAV mode has a page that shows your groundspeed, bearing, distance, track made good, ETE, and ETA, plus a CDI with a digital display of crosstrack error. Also displayed is the word ODD or EVEN, depending on your bearing, as a reminder of the appropriate cruising altitude (not really necessary if you're still walking).

A "vertical info" page, which is a simple type of VNAV function, shows the altitude change you must make, in feet, to get to the TO waypoint, along with the necessary angle of descent or ascent. This is not very useful, since both the pilot and his VSI operate in terms of feet per minute.

The NEAR mode, as expected, enables you to observe your bearing and distance to the 10 airports, VORs, and user waypoints closest to your present position *or* those that are closest to any other waypoint you select (a handy way of choosing an alternate destination if the need arises). It would be nice if the display included the facility name, but all you get is the identifier.

Time, Timing, and Trips

The TIME mode displays the date and time, as well as three independent timers, which can be set to count up or down.

The TRIP mode is one you may never use; it's mostly for mariners and/or compulsive diarists. It will display such riveting data on your current trip as: the total distance and time you have traveled, expressed in miles, hours, and days; the highest and lowest altitudes you have achieved; current, average, and maximum speed; and if that's not enough, the distance you've covered from your starting point to your present position—including turns and other excursions—plus the average direction of your flight! Actually, that's a bit more than I would want to know, but there it is.

There's MORE

The MORE mode provides you with considerable data on the status of the satellites the sensor is either receiving or searching for, including the satellite's identification number, signal status, elevation angle, azimuth, and user range accuracy.

A "From A to B" screen enables you to determine the bearing and range between any two waypoints in the database. True airspeed, density, and wind computations are made in this mode.

Also, the MORE mode allows you to customize various displays, such as clock style (12- or 24-hour); date format; time zone; units of altitude, distance, and speed; CDI scale. You can find out when the sun will rise and set any day, anywhere. You can adjust the screen contrast as well as turn on the backlighting.

If you are operating with the battery pack, you can choose between the maximum rate, which updates every second-and-a-half, and the battery saver rate, which updates every five seconds (and is rather lethargic for aircraft speeds). Battery life is estimated to be four to five hours at the maximum rate and five to ten hours at the battery saver rate.

When the Flightmate's sensor thinks the batteries are low, a massive warning message is flashed on the screen every so often (*too* often). I have found the sensor to be on the pessimistic side, broadcasting premature obituaries about batteries that still show vital life signs when prodded by my tester.

My Impressions

I believe that the Flightmate will appeal primarily to the budget-conscious pilot who does not want or need some features found in higher-priced models.

Its display is the smallest of the current crop, although it is quite readable. And its database is stark, lacking the airport comm frequencies, runway information, etc., that is provided in the other models (except for GARMIN's 55 AVD that is also plain and considerably more expensive).

All in all, the Flightmate does a perfectly good job of navigating, and if you're willing to accept a few limitations in exchange for a friendlier depletion of the piggy bank, the Flightmate could suit you just fine. The Pro lists for $995. And there's a plainer-still version, the Pro SE (for Sport Edition), listing for $795. It is similar to the regular Pro, except that it does not have a data port, and the battery eliminator and remote antenna are optional, at $90 and $125 respectively. (A Trimble spokesman told me that the unit, when mounted on the yoke, will receive four satellites with just the built-in antenna.)

Incidentally, there's a Trimble handheld with moving map display in the works, as one might expect.

Magellan

The MAP 7000 features a moving map display; it replaces Magellan's mapless NAV 5000 handheld. The MAP 7000 has a detachable antenna that can be suction-cupped to the windshield and a keypad control system. Airports and VORs are contained in an internal database, with a choice of North America or International coverage. Updates are performed at the factory at a cost of $150.

There is memory for 500 user waypoints, which can be depicted on the map as intersections, and 20 flight plans with up to 25 legs apiece.

Airports can be called up by identifier or city name. Airport information includes frequencies and runway diagram, length, surface, and lighting.

The map display has five scales, ranging from 10 to 250 nm. I have not used the MAP 7000 at this writing, but based on my experience with other moving map displays, I would want to be able to access scales smaller than 10 nm, for greater detail when approaching a destination airport.

Magellan's MAP 7000 replaces the mapless NAV 5000 handheld. It's a middle-of-the-road unit, in terms of both price and features.

Magellan has chosen not to incorporate an arrival mode, on the theory that pilots might use it to shoot approaches in poor visibility, which could be unsafe if the GPS signals were being degraded by the Department of Defense's Selective Availability procedure. As a compromise of sorts, the set can display an airport's runway diagram, while a bug at the screen's border indicates the plane's approximate bearing to that airport.

Class B and C airspace is depicted in the form of circles.

Other features of the unit include winds aloft computations, fuel planning, VNAV, and a Morse code display for VORs. There's also a rather limited demo mode; it allows you to view the map at any starting position you select, but there is no motion and you'll be given a bearing and distance only to the pre-set destination of Lakeland, Florida. (Well, that'll come in handy whenever you go to Sun 'n Fun.)

Dimensions: 8.75" H x 3.5" W x 2.13" D. Price: $1,299, which includes a yoke mount and cigarette lighter adapter. The NAV 5000A can be upgraded to a MAP 7000 for $400.

Sony

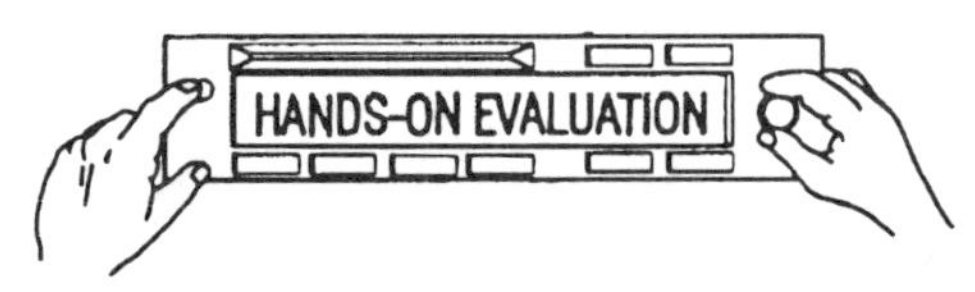

Quite a stir of interest ensued when the powerful Japanese electronics manufacturer introduced its first handheld GPS receiver, the PYXIS IPS-360. However, for the aviation market at least, the set was a total disaster. In the previous edition of this book, I referred to it as "an exercise in exasperation."

Then Sony produced—a bit too hastily—a successor model, the IPS-760. It was withdrawn briefly for some much-needed modifications and now is back with us.

The unit has an 8-channel GPS sensor and a detachable antenna. It provides the largest display of any of the handhelds to date and offers moving map capability.

Dimensions are 8.9" H x 4.2" W x 1.3" D. Power is provided by 6 AA alkaline batteries, with a rechargeable battery kit and cigarette lighter adapter available as options. The unit is controlled by a variety of dedicated mode keys, multi-function "soft" keys, and cursor arrow keys.

There are slots for *two* data packs, each of which is about one third the size of a

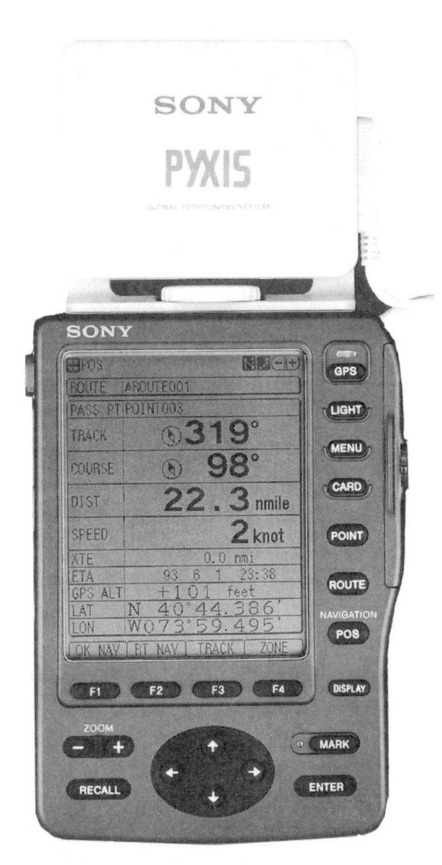

Sony's IPS-760 has a large display and user-replaceable data cards, but is not easy to operate.

conventional data card. One slot holds a data pack with coverage of either North America or the rest of the world. The database consists of airports, VORs, and NDBs, including radio frequencies, runway information, etc. Also shown are the outer boundaries of Class B and C airspace, plus state lines, major rivers, and country boundaries. The second pack depicts the Class B and C altitude segments. The packs are supplied by ARNAV Systems, which offers updates at $179 per pack.

There is memory for 1,000 user waypoints and 50 routes.

My Impressions

Although this set is a vast improvement over the IPS-360, it is by no means user-friendly; the word *cumbersome* comes readily to mind. With some practice, you should be able to navigate from Point A to Point B, but creating a flight plan is a real piece of work, and forget about editing it if you need to amend your route while in flight.

It is obvious that the IPS-760's operating system was designed by people who were never faced with the prospect of using it in the dynamics of the real world. This is truly unfortunate, because the unit, with its removable data packs and large display, offers impressive potential. If Sony were to take it back to the drawing board again and make some truly intelligent changes, the set would be worthy of serious consideration. But in its present form, I feel that it is just too much of a hassle. Price: $1,599.

More Handhelds to Come

As this book was going to press, I learned that two other GPS handheld receivers were scheduled for production. One is being manufactured by Trimble and the other by Lowrance Avionics. The latter company is a division of Lowrance Electronics, a manufacturer that is already producing GPS handhelds for other applications and is now entering the aviation market.

At this writing, no reliable details were available on the new units, but they may be in production by the time you read this. And in time, you can expect to see even more models, presumably until some saturation point is reached.

11

Various Types of Moving Map Systems

In the preceding two chapters, we saw a number of GPS receivers that have built-in moving map displays. Now we are going to look at different types of moving map systems. Some are panel-mounted units, while others consist of software packages designed to turn portable personal computers into moving map systems. The advantage of the latter system is that you get, in addition to moving map capability, all of the other functions inherent in a PC—plus a display that's as large as that particular computer's screen. But consider that you have to position the computer where you can operate it and view its display without it getting in the way. (A product called Tripboard, marketed by Flight Products International of Kalispell, MT, might serve this purpose; it lists for $145.) Also, the computer's battery duration will have to be adequate for your needs.

A note of caution: Some of the software providers are small outfits, with all of the know-how residing in the head of one person. More than once I have telephoned with a question or a problem, only to be told that, "He's on a trip and nobody else can help you." If you can live with that kind of response, fine; otherwise, you'd be well advised to check on the company's product support capability before you buy.

All of these systems must be interfaced with a source of position information. This could be a compatible GPS or loran receiver with a serial data port, or simply a barebones remote sensor. Your choice would depend on the functions you want. Bear in mind that the moving map system has its own database, so if you connect it to a GPS or loran receiver that also has a database, you will have two databases to update.

Let's begin our product reviews with the manufacturer that gave general aviation its first practical moving map display.

Eventide

It is interesting to note that some of the most innovative avionics equipment has come to us from sources other than the traditional avionics manufacturers.

The first line of reasonably priced moving map displays was brought to market by an electronics equipment manufacturer called Eventide. The company offers three models: the Argus 3000, 5000, and 7000. The 3000 is a basic model designed for the VFR pilot. The step-up 5000 has the same dimensions and virtually the same appearance as the 3000, with the addition of features that will appeal to the IFR pilot. The top-of-the-line 7000 is larger than the other two models and has other distinctions as well.

Since all three models perform in much the same way, I'll describe the functions as they are found in the 5000, which I have in my Tiger—and then I'll explain the differences that occur in the other models.

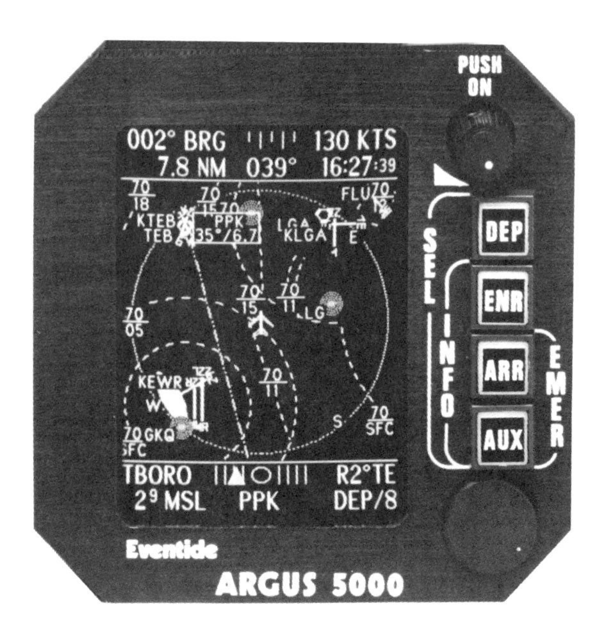

Even though the Argus 5000's screen is fairly small, the information it presents is quite legible—especially at the lower ranges.

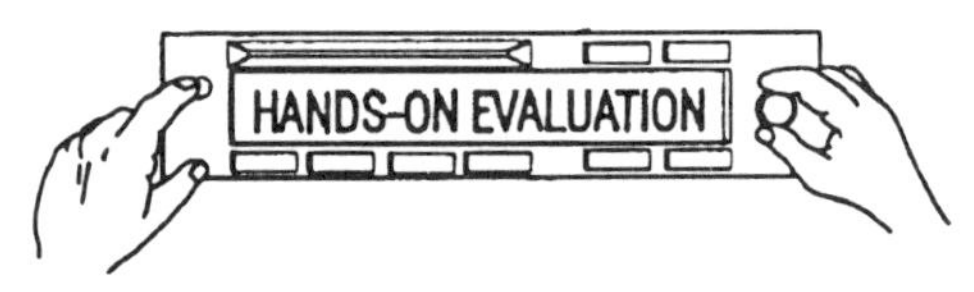

The **5000** fits into a 3-inch square panel cutout. That includes the CRT—which displays its graphics in green on a black background—plus the controls, consisting of an on-off/dimmer knob and four mode selector buttons.

The 5000's database contains airports with runways of 2000 feet or longer, VORs, NDBs, and fan markers. Intersections, heliports, and seaplane bases are available as options, for a one-time charge.

Airport information includes the name and identifier; city; latitude and longitude coordinates; frequencies for the ATIS, approach control, tower and ground control; field elevation; magnetic variation; runway length, lighting and width; instrument approaches; and available fuel types.

The database covers the entire US, including Alaska and Hawaii, plus the Virgin Islands, Puerto Rico, and portions of Canada. An international database is offered as a $500 option.

Eventide has recently added the option of creating and storing flight plans in the Argus itself. The manufacturer suggests that flight planning should be easier with the Argus because it is more likely to be located directly in front of the pilot than a GPS or loran receiver. That seems logical, but the downside is that creating flight plans is more cumbersome in the Argus than in most GPS and loran sets.

Due to memory limitations, the number of flight plans that can be stored in the Argus depends on the number of user waypoints that have been stored, and vice versa.

The cost of the flight planning software is $750 for sets manufactured on or after June 30, 1993, and $1,000 for older units.

The database is updatable by the user. However, the process is not a simple matter of sliding in a replacement card or cartridge, as is the case with some lorans and GPS models. The 5000's database is on a circuit card, and you'll need a screwdriver plus a little patience to make the exchange. Updates are available every 56 days by subscription or on a one-time basis.

The outlines and notations of all types of special use airspace are depicted. Upper and lower segments of the CRT provide such information as distance, bearing, groundspeed, heading, ETA, and minimum safe altitude. A course deviation indicator is also displayed.

Departure, Enroute, and Arrival Modes

The set has three operating modes and several submodes. The major modes are *departure, enroute,* and *arrival.*

When you select the *departure* mode, the symbolic airplane is shown in the center of the screen, in a "heading up" display that includes all landing facilities within the selected range. Ranges from 1 to 40 nm can be chosen. The "heading up" display means that if, for example, an airport is at your plane's two o'clock position, that's where it will appear relative to the symbolic airplane on the screen. If you turn the plane to head directly to that airport, the moving map will also turn until the airport symbol is at the aircraft symbol's 12 o'clock position, and so on.

The *enroute* mode moves the symbolic aircraft down the screen to provide an 80 percent forward view and a 20 percent aft view. Selectable ranges in this mode are from 1 to 240 nm. Like the departure mode, the enroute mode has a "heading up" orientation.

The *arrival* mode is a "north up" display, with ranges of 2 nm to 40 nm. In this mode, the background is stationary and the symbolic aircraft moves in accordance with the loran or GPS input. This is useful in approaching an airport, in that the runways are shown on the display with their magnetic orientation.

An *information* submode provides such data as airport lat/lon, runway widths and lengths, frequencies, lighting, etc. Then there is an *emergency* submode that will display radial and distance information to the five nearest landing facilities.

The 5000 can be given heading sense if it's interfaced with a compatible DG or HSI (with ARINC 407 synchro output). This means that the map display will turn almost instantaneously with the airplane. Without this interface, the 5000 relies entirely on the loran or GPS for its track information. With a loran receiver, this results in a certain amount of time lag while the set updates its position. GPS receivers update more rapidly, and the time lag is negligible.

An internal real-time clock provides your ETA to the active waypoint.

ADF and Stormscope Displays Available

Short on panel space? You can install the 5000 in place of your remote ADF indicator; the Argus system will superimpose a heading-oriented ADF display on the moving map display—*provided* your ADF box is compatible. Most are; those that are *not* include the Bendix/King KR 86, Narco ADF 841 and the Bendix T12B, C, and D units. (However, I was able to get my Narco ADF 841 modified to work with the 5000.)

An RMI adapter allows you to display two VOR pointers or one VOR and one ADF pointer on the Argus screen. The adapter is priced at $1,495 for the 5000 and 7000, and $2,250 for the 3000.

Owners of some Stormscope models can save yet another panel hole. An optional weather display adapter allows you to switch from the moving map display to the Stormscope weather dots, all on the Argus' screen.

The weather display adapter attaches to the back of the 5000 or can be remotely mounted. It lists for $995, and is available also for the 3000 and 7000.

Eventually, the Argus will be compatible, without an adapter, with Insight's Strike Finder weather avoidance system—which should be on the market again, now that the legal thunder with Stormscope is beginning to dissipate.

The 5000 is TSOd and IFR certified. List price for the basic system is $4,995.

As I indicated, I have an Argus 5000 in my plane. When I first saw that display, I thought it would be too small to be really useful. Not so. The trick, when in the enroute mode, is to use fairly small ranges; I keep it in the 30 nm range a good deal of the time. Larger ranges become too cluttered, especially in high density areas. True, you can deselect from the screen such depictions as navaids, airports, and special use airspace, but I like to keep them up there.

The CRT's definition is quite good, and with judicious use of the dimming control, the screen remains readable under virtually all conditions.

Watch the SUAs Go By

I live near a smorgasbord of SUAs, and it's comforting to look at the 5000's display and watch a blob of Class B airspace slide harmlessly to one side of the airplane symbol as I maneuver around it. Even the various altitude sectors are shown.

Finding an airport and lining up with the right runway in murky weather is made easier via the 5000's approach mode.

I have the weather display adapter hooked up to my Stormscope WX-11 and that works out pretty well. However, I was disappointed to find that when I switch the Stormscope display on, it takes the place of the Argus display and vice versa. Somehow, I thought the weather dots would be superimposed on the moving map, (and so have others with whom I've discussed this), but such is not the case. I wish that at the very least, Eventide would design an annunciation that would alert the pilot when Stormscope dots are forming while he is watching the moving map display.

How do I like the Argus 5000? I like it just fine. To me, it's another one of those panel embellishments without which I managed to struggle through the skies for several decades, but now would hate to give up.

The **3000**, as I mentioned earlier, is virtually identical in appearance to the 5000; there is a minor cosmetic difference in that the latter's knob and mode button bezels are black, while on the 3000 they're gray.

"I can live with that," I hear you say. However, cosmetic surgery was not the only operation performed. A scalpel was wielded on the inside, and here's what got removed:

Real-time clock. Instead of ETA, you get ETE.

Gyrocompass heading information. The deletion of that circuitry means that you can't interface the 3000 with a DG or HSI.

ADF display. The 3000 cannot be interfaced with an ADF, so you don't get that saving in panel space.

User-updatable database. The 3000 must be sent back to the factory whenever a database update is desired. The present cost of an update is $200. The 3000's database does not have the intersection and heliport options, but the seaplane bases are included at no extra charge. Also, the airport data has been expanded to include fields with runways that are 1600 feet or longer.

Integration with a variety of long range navigation systems. The 3000 gets its position only from loran. It is not designed to interface with flight management systems, VLF Omega, or inertial systems. (I'll bet most of you can live with *that*, too.)

TSO and IFR certification. The 3000 has not been put through the testing and procedures necessary to earn those FAA diplomas. However, Eventide states that "although the Argus 3000 is not TSOd, it meets the DO-160B environmental standards in terms of altitude, heat, vibration, etc. It is every bit as reliable and rugged as is the TSOd Argus 5000."

So there you have the essential differences between the 3000 and the 5000, plus the former's considerably lower list price of $2,995.

The 7000 is designed for the corporate market. The unit is 4 ¼" H x 3" W, and has a screen whose size is 1.72 times that of the 3000 and 5000. The control buttons are arranged horizontally below the CRT,

CRT, and the database is accessed from the front. In other respects, the system functions like a 5000. List price: $6,995.

Eventide plans to offer a remote GPS sensor and antenna for use with all of its systems.

ARNAV

The **MFD 5000** is referred to by ARNAV as a cockpit management system. It has a monochrome CRT display, approximately 4.25" W x 3" H.

In addition to a moving map, the MFD 5000 has an optional EICAS (engine indication and crew alert system) display. In plain English, this means that engine instrumentation can be displayed on the screen and an alert message will appear (along with an audio signal) if there's an out-of-range condition, such as an overly high cylinder head temperature.

Sensors include heading; fuel level, flow, and pressure; EGT; CHT; oil pressure and temperature; manifold pressure; electrical load; vacuum; angle of attack; and more, for as many as 35 engine and airframe conditions.

The moving map display utilizes a Jeppesen user-replaceable database that contains airports, VORs, NDBs, intersections, airways, Class B and C airspace boundaries, SIDs, STARs, and approaches. In addition, there's digital elevation mapping, man-made obstructions,

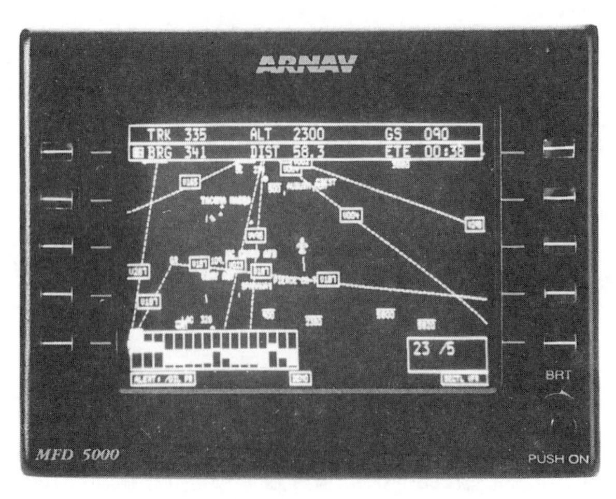

ARNAV's MFD 5000 has a large screen and shows such details as highways, terrain elevations, and man-made obstructions.

highways, and more.

An advisory function compares the aircraft's altitude to the digital elevation database and alerts the pilot if he goes below minimum safe altitude.

The complete system consists of three units: the MFD 5000 CDU (control/display unit, measuring 6.25" W x 4.75" H x 8.9" D; the panel-mounted LRU (line replaceable unit) 5010, which contains the database card reader and measures 6.25" W x 2" H x 9.25" D; and the remote-mounted LRU 5020 EICAS processor, measuring 6" W x 1.125" H x 6" D.

Base price of the MFD 5000 is $4,995. The EICAS system is priced at $2,495, not including sensors.

Peacock

The **LapMap** is a package that turns any laptop computer into a moving map system. It consists of a database and utility programs, plus a data cable that connects your laptop computer to your loran or GPS. The LapMap display includes airports, VORs, NDBs, intersections, user waypoints, special use airspace (including Class B altitude sectors), ATAs, a ground track, and a course line.

Displayed information includes bearing and distance; ETE; ETA; groundspeed; ground track; VNAV; airport frequencies, elevation, and

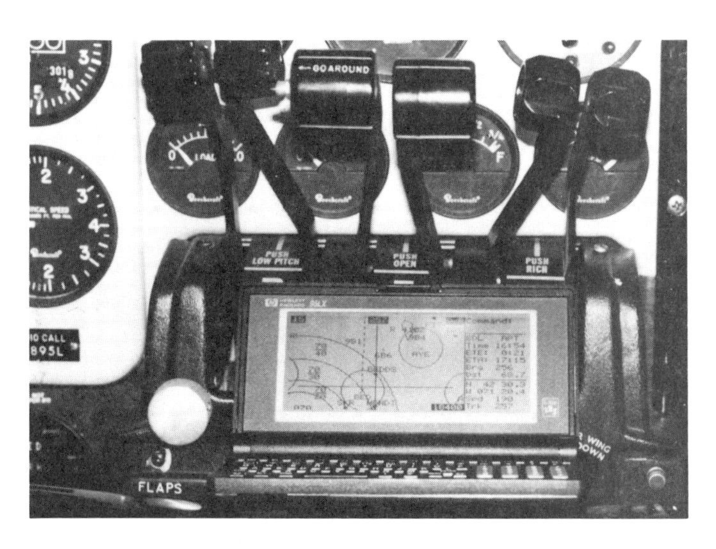

This location for a LapMap looks pretty good—provided you don't have to cage an engine in a hurry.

runway information; winds aloft; and wind correction angle. There's a North-up arrival mode, and airport runways are depicted.

The beauty of the LapMap concept is that you get more than a moving map system—you get a computer you can use for other purposes, including accessing DUAT even when you're on a trip.

The price of the LapMap package is $695, including one update. You can order a one-year subscription consisting of two updates for $89, or updates on a 56-day basis for $249. The updates include any program enhancements that are developed. Peacock also supplies packages that include computers.

The **GPS 5000** is a remote-mounted 5-channel GPS receiver that Peacock is offering for $995, plus $395 for your choice of windshield or external antenna. This can be interfaced with the Hewlett-Packard 100LX palmtop computer for a total cost, including all necessary software and hardware, of under $2,600.

Zycom

The **AEROplan** is a portable computer with an aviation database and moving map software. The AEROplan GPS V package includes a Rockwell 5-channel GPS sensor and antenna. The system is powered by a cigarette lighter adapter.

The computer measures 7.5" W x 4" H x 1" D; its display area is about 5" W x 1.5" H. The unit is controlled by a membrane keypad. The database contains US airports, VORs, NDBs, intersections, and airways. Airport information includes city, state, frequencies, runway layouts, lighting, fuel, ILS availability, elevation, and pattern altitude.

Map scales range from 2 to 2000 nm. With optional sensors, the screen can display a variety of fuel and temperature conditions.

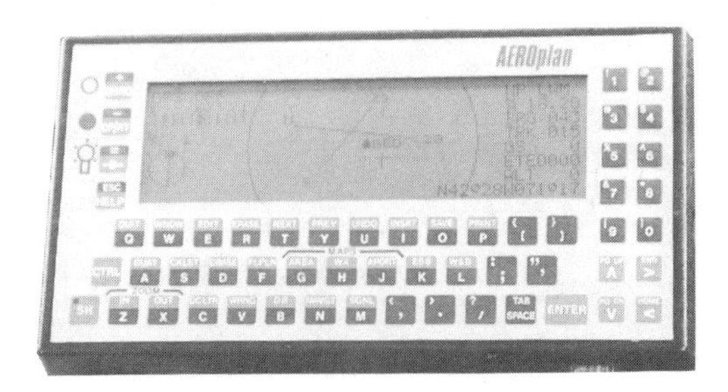

Zycom claims that AEROplan can provide output to an autopilot.

There is memory for 300 user waypoints and 30 flight plans of up to 169 legs total. A search function looks for the seven nearest airports. The computer contains a modem.

The AEROplan computer with software lists for $1,198; with the GPS V receiver, the price is $1,699. An economy version, including the GPS V receiver, but without the modem and certain software features, is priced at $1,295.

Memtec

Memtec offers a choice of handheld and remote moving map systems with an optional 6-channel GPS sensor.

The **Co-Pilot** handheld is 4.75" W x 10" H x 1.63" D and contains a NiCad battery pack; it can also be operated with a cigarette lighter adapter.

Its database covers the continental US and includes all public use and military airports, VORs, and NDBs. Airport information includes frequencies, beacon, runway lighting and surface, and fuel availability.

Flight planning capability includes route calculations, checklists, weight and balance calculations, and route and approach timing. A dead reckoning mode will drive the moving map without a loran or GPS receiver. (This, of course, will be subject to much larger position errors than those resulting from loran or GPS input.)

The map display includes the outlines of Class B, C, and D airspace, as well as airports and navaids. Scales range from 7 to 60 nm; runways are depicted in the 7 nm scale.

The Co-Pilot is priced at $799 without the GPS sensor and $1,195

Memtec offers a remotely operated model, as shown here, plus a handheld.

with the sensor.

The **Co-Pilot Remote** measures 4⅝" W x 5½" H x 6½" D and the display is 3" x 4". The set is operated by a remote control unit. The price is $995 without the GPS sensor and $1,395 with the sensor. Memtec also provides moving map software for use with a PC, priced at $175. The manufacturer offers a 30-day money-back guarantee.

MentorPlus

FliteMap moving map software is provided for PC and Macintosh laptop and notebook computers that meet the required specifications. In addition, MentorPlus offers an optional flat panel display for more convenient placement in the cockpit. The panel measures 10.5" W x 7" H x 1" D and the display area is about 7¾" x 5¾". The panel has its own power supply with cigarette lighter adapter and interfaces with PC (but not Mac) computers.

There is a choice of North America, European, and international databases. Included are airports, VORs, NDBs, and intersections. All types of special use airspace are depicted, including Class B and C floors and ceilings.

According to the company, an "unlimited" number of flight plans, legs, and user waypoints can be stored.

Map scales range from 0.5 to 300 nm. A data window at the bottom of the map shows bearing, distance, and ETE to the nearest airport, nearest VOR, next waypoint, and destination waypoint. Extended airport data can be called up, including frequencies, the longest runway; pattern altitude; availability of fuel, oxygen, and repairs.

Other functions include VNAV, E-6B computations, and a flight data recorder.

FliteMap is priced at $395 with the North America database; the European and international databases list for $595 and $995 respectively. The flat panel with FliteMap is $1,695. MentorPlus also produces FliteStar flight planning software at prices ranging from $295 to $895, depending on database geographical coverage.

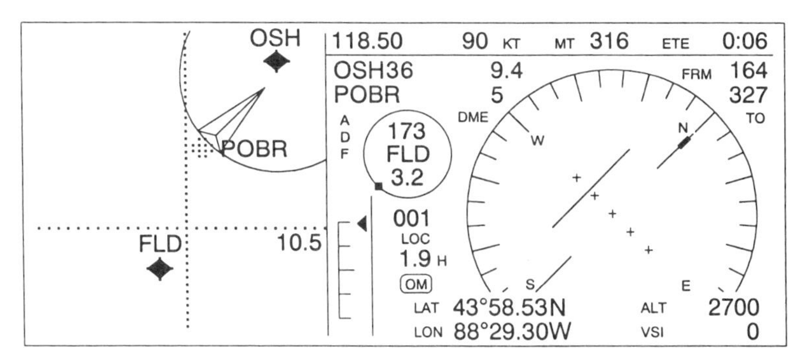

Genese's Glassnav program displays an electronic HSI and RMI for position awareness.

Genese

The **Glassnav** moving map program can be purchased with a variety of hardware options. The program's database includes US public use airports, VORs, NDBs, and special use airspace. Major airport runways are shown graphically. Position awareness is depicted by an electronic HSI and RMI. Features include an electronically generated glideslope and localizer simulation, and vertical guidance is provided down to 600 feet above the runway elevation.

In regard to these simulated landing navaids, I want to emphasize that software programs by Genese and other providers are not FAA certified and are not to be used for IFR operations or relied on in conditions of poor visibility.

Glassnav is priced at $395. Options include an HP-95LX palmtop computer at $399, a flash memory card at $359, and an interface cable at $35. Genese offers several packages that include a 6-channel GPS receiver, controller, and other components, at prices ranging from $1,795 to $3,195.

In the next chapter, we'll take a look at other types of equipment that can be interfaced with those GPS and loran receivers that have data ports.

12

GPS & Loran Accessories

As I noted in the previous chapter, those GPS and loran sets that have data ports can interface with moving map systems to bring an extra dimension to your navigation. There are other products that also connect with GPS and loran receivers, and there will be more of them in the future. Here's a look at the equipment that's available now.

Fuel Computers

Since a GPS or loran receiver knows the aircraft's groundspeed and distance to the waypoint, it can combine this information with a fuel computer's knowledge of fuel flow and fuel remaining. Result: a computation that tells you whether or not you'll get there with fuel to spare—assuming, of course, that you enter the correct fuel quantity at each pit stop.

Shadin's Digiflo-L, Microflo-L, and Miniflo-L models work with the GPS or loran unit to display fuel required to reach the waypoint. When the mode switch is in either the fuel-to-destination or fuel-reserve mode, the display will flash if the fuel remaining drops below a 45-minute reserve, or if you program a waypoint that is beyond reach. The instruments also compute specific range in miles per gallon or pound.

The Digiflo-L fits in a 3⅛" hole. Price: $1,890 (single) and $2,395 (twin). The Microflo-L is made for a 2¼" cutout. Price: $1,665 (single) and $2,100 (twin). The Miniflo-L is in a flatpack configuration, 1.25" H x 3.25" W. Price: $1,550 (single) and $1,999 (twin). An EGT version of the Miniflo-L displays exhaust gas temperature instead of a projection of the fuel quantity remaining at your destination. Single-probe price is $1,665 (single) and $2,100 (twin). Multiple-probe units are also available. All of these prices are for typical installations, including transducer(s) and harness.

ARNAV's FC-10 combines with the GPS or loran unit for a display of absolute range—that is, how many nautical miles you can fly until the tanks run dry. The unit fits into a 2¼" hole. The single-engine model is priced at $1,495; the multi-engine version is $2,195.

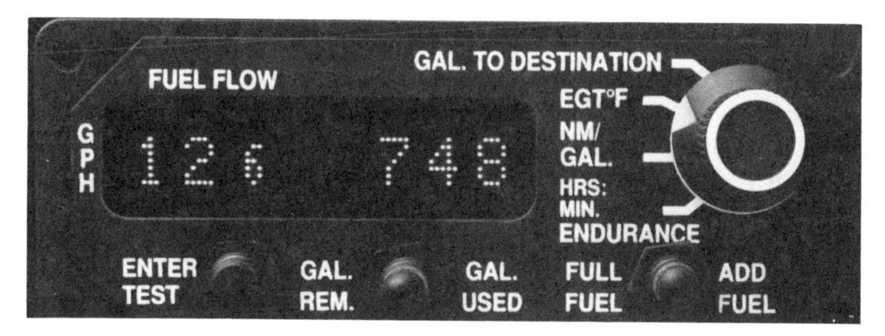

You can choose between two Shadin Miniflo-L displays: projected fuel quantity at destination or, as shown above, exhaust gas temperature.

Fuel/Air Data System

Shadin's F/ADC fuel/air data system is a remote-mounted box with a variety of sensors. It enables a compatible GPS or loran receiver to display true airspeed, pressure and density altitude, true outside air temperature, and winds aloft—all automatically, without any pilot input. With a fuel transducer as part of the system, the F/ADC functions as a fuel flow sensor in order to provide the following information: fuel flow rate; fuel required to reach the destination waypoint; fuel remaining; fuel efficiency, in nautical miles per gallon; absolute range; range remaining; fuel on board at arrival; fuel reserve at arrival; time reserve at arrival; and total fuel used.

In addition, the F/ADC provides automatic altitude input for GPS navigation when only three satellites are in view. Price: $2,550.

Serializer

This remote-mounted unit interfaces with your altitude encoder to transmit your transponder's Mode C output to your GPS receiver and thus provide automatic altitude input when only three satellites are in view.

Icarus makes a Model 3000 serializer that works with every GPS unit. Price: $295.

Emergency Locator Transmitter

A GPS or loran receiver knows the aircraft's position, so it makes sense to interface it with an ELT, which can transmit that position to rescuers in the event of a crash.

Artex Aircraft Supplies' ELS-10 is a talking ELT. If it is activated by an impact, a voice synthesizer broadcasts the plane's tail number, time of activation, and position in lat/lon. The ELS-10 has been certified to C91A, the latest ELT TSO, with stringent standards that are designed to eliminate false alarms. This unit was originally manufactured by ARNAV. Price: $895.

Course Deviation Indicators

Virtually all GPS and loran sets have their own built-in electronic CDI display for steering guidance. Nevertheless, there are some external CDIs on the market that are designed specifically to work with GPS and loran receivers.

A major advantage of this type of instrument over the receiver's own CDI is that it usually can be located more directly in your line of vision than a GPS or loran set that is in the radio stack. Also, this arrangement frees up the receiver's display for other information.

But why not install a switching arrangement that enables you to use your #1 or #2 VOR receiver's CDI (or HSI) for either VOR/LOC or loran/GPS steering information? Actually, a lot of pilots, including this writer, do just that—and, in fact, that's the only way to get the GPS or loran receiver to drive an autopilot. However, a number of VOR/LOC CDIs are not designed to accept GPS or loran input—including several that are used with some popular Bendix/King nav/comms.

There is also the possibility that if one CDI is shared by a VOR and a GPS or loran receiver, a pilot might become confused about which type of nav information he's looking at.

In addition, the external GPS and loran CDIs have built-in lights for such annunciations as: WARN (unusable signal), ARIV (arriving at the waypoint), APR (utilizing approach mode), PTK (utilizing parallel track), and VFR (signal not suitable for IFR). The types of annunciations vary from model to model. Incidentally, certain annunciations are required for IFR-certified lorans, but they need not be incorporated into a CDI.

BVR offers more than 20 TSOd models; they can be specifically tailored to the GPS or loran that has been installed. Prices range from $650 to $750.

Mid-Continent provides TSOd CDIs for all GPS and loran models in both 2¼" round and flatpack 1" H x 2.5" W x 3.5" D. Prices range from $525 to $655.

Mid-Continent's MD 40-60 has annunciations for parallel track, warn, approach, and waypoint.

Now it's time to take a look at those good old standbys, the VHF nav and comm radios. Actually, most current versions of these sets are using microprocessor technology and are quite sophisticated—as you'll see in the next two chapters.

13

Features to Consider in VHF Navs & Comms

The nav/comms may not be as sexy as the highly computerized GPS and loran receivers, but there are still quite a few design considerations and operational features to be aware of when making your choice.

Stand-Alone or All-In-One?

Some nav receivers and comm transceivers are designed as stand-alone units—that is, each is complete in itself, with no shared components. A stand-alone nav together with a stand-alone comm is known as a "1 + 1" system.

Then there's the design that combines the nav and the comm in one box. This is the "1 + ½" system, so-called because the nav and the comm use the same power supply and certain other components. The 1 + ½ radio is popular because it takes up less panel space than most 1 + 1 systems (the Terra "mini-models" being a notable exception).

The 1 + 1 system has the advantage of redundancy: if the 1 + ½ system's power supply fails, you've lost the whole works, whereas with a 1 + 1 system, one of the boxes will continue to function.

Then there is the economy "shared receiver" system, typified by the Narco Escort II. Like the 1 + ½ systems, this equipment combines both nav and comm radios in one box, but since they share a single receiver, you can't use both capabilities at the same time. For example, if you're navigating from a VOR and want to talk to a controller, you'll lose the VOR steering information when you switch to the comm side—and vice versa.

This type of unit is not recommended as a primary radio, except possibly for the pilot who flies only in the sunshine and does not wander into unfamiliar high-density controlled airspace. However, it is also worth considering as a low-cost backup to a more sophisticated nav/comm system.

Size & Shape

While most of the panel-mounted loran sets have settled into the 2" H x 6.25" W footprint, the navs, comms, and nav/comms come in a variety of dimensions. An imaginative use of the available configurations could help you to squeeze the optimum amount of avionics into limited panel space. See the next chapter for specifics.

Displays and Frequency Management

Although a few models are still being produced with the old-style mechanical displays, most have the more modern electronic digital readouts. The latter may be LCD, LED, gas discharge, or incandescent.

Most of these sets also have the capability of storing one or more frequencies in memory, which can ease the pilot's workload. A typical example is the popular "flip-flop" system used on the current Bendix/King and Narco nav/comms. On both the nav and comm sides, there is an active frequency window and a standby frequency window. A new frequency is usually entered in the standby window. When the pilot wants to activate that frequency, he presses a transfer button and the frequencies change sides: the standby frequency goes into the active window and the active frequency obligingly takes its position in the standby window. That way, if a controller gives you a change of frequency and you either copied it wrong or for some other reason don't get a response on the new frequency, simply press the transfer button again and you're back on the previous frequency.

Then there are the radios that can store more than one standby frequency. For example, Bendix/King's KY 96A and KY 196A hold nine frequencies, Narco's Mark 12D+ will accommodate 10, the TKM MX-170 and MX-300 store 50, and the McCoy digital modification of the King KX 170/175 radios can warehouse 60 comm and 60 nav frequencies.

With extra storage capability, you can pre-program ATIS, clearance delivery, ground control, tower, and departure control from your departure airport, as well as the appropriate frequencies at your destination. Then just punch them up in sequence as you need them. Some sets even have an optional remote frequency transfer button that can be installed on the yoke.

Bendix/King's KLX 135 GPS/Comm and Northstar's SmartComm use GPS input to provide easy access to frequencies of facilities near your plane's present position. For details, see the chapter entitled "A New Breed: GPS/Comms."

The electronic display can be designed to show more than frequencies. Some sets, such as the Bendix/King KX 165 and Narco Mark 12D+, have a "digital RMI" feature that provides a readout of the airplane's bearing to or radial from the VOR in use. This is especially helpful when you are navigating to IFR fixes that are defined by radials.

A Talking Nav/Comm

McCoy's 1700V model is blessed with the power of speech. A synthesized voice announces both the active and standby frequencies at the press of a button. The voice will also keep you verbally advised of the time remaining on the countdown timer—a convenient reminder during IFR approaches.

ECDIs

Electronic course deviation indicators show crosstrack error via light bars instead of needles. The light bars radiate from the center of the display either to the left or right—as well as up or down if there is glideslope capability—and you "fly to the light bars" in the same way that you fly to the needle with an analog CDI.

Some ECDIs have digital RMI, timer, and automatic radial centering functions. Automatic radial centering allows the pilot to center the left-right needle or light bars at the press of a button, eliminating the need to manually turn the OBS.

Well, there you have the major bells and whistles you can choose from in today's high-tech nav/comms. We'll take a look at the specific models in the chapter that follows.

14

Panel-Mounted VHF Navs & Comms

Nothing in the world of navs and comms can match the excitement of loran and GPS, but the last few years have seen increased frequency storage capability—and some bargain prices! Here are product descriptions of the panel-mounted navigation, communication, and combined nav/comm units, grouped by manufacturer.

Note: The more recent comm sets are designed with 760-channel capability, to utilize 40 new channels that are being allocated gradually for ATIS, AWOS, ATC, and unicom communications. I have noted 760 channels where applicable; the other models have 720 channels. On the nav side, 200 channels remains the standard.

Also, the nav/comm units are 1 + ½ systems unless otherwise noted.

Bendix/King

Bendix/King traditionally has designated its radios as either the commercial Gold Crown series or the general aviation Silver Crown series. Now the company has added a just plain Crown series. (I guess they didn't want to call it Plastic Crown.) It consists of a group of former Silver Crown sets that have been given the manufacturer's regal dispensation to be installed by the owner (the other radios must be installed by an authorized dealer for the warranty to be valid), as long as the selling dealer provides an installation manual and is available for technical assistance.

The Crown radios have been re-styled to match the new KLX 135 GPS/Comm transceiver; operationally they are unchanged. Those Crown models that are covered in this book include, in addition to the KLX 135, the KX 125 nav/comm and the KY 96A/97A comm transceivers.

With its built-in CDI, the KX 125 saves both space and money.

The **KX 125** is Bendix/King's newest and lowest-price panel-mounted nav/comm. It has 760 comm channels and an LCD display with flip-flop tuning and direct tuning of the active frequency. The set has remote frequency transfer capability (via a button mounted on the yoke), as do other Bendix/King nav/comms. Another KX 125 feature that applies to other Bendix/King sets is a non-volatile memory circuit that stores the frequencies in memory during power shutdowns without a connection to the aircraft battery.

The KX 125 has a built-in VOR/LOC indicator, with automatic centering of the VOR in use. You can toggle between the CDI and a digital readout of radial or bearing. The set can also interface with an external CDI, as well as current Bendix/King DME and glideslope equipment. Transmitter output: 5W. Dimensions: 2" H x 6.25" W x 10.16" D. Price: $2,062.

The **KX 155** nav/comm has a gas discharge digital display and flip- flop tuning. Transmitter output: 10W. Dimensions: 2" H x 6.26" W x 10.16" D. Price without glideslope: $3,725. With glideslope: $4,343. Prices include indicators with "windshield wiper" action. Package prices with higher quality rectilinear indicators are $4,331 and $5,000 respectively.

The **KX 165** is a step-up model, with the same transmitter output and dimensions as the KX 155. This set will display the aircraft's radial from the VOR in use. In addition, it has a built-in VOR/LOC converter, whereas the KX 155 does not. Sold only with glideslope: $6,777. Rectilinear indicators are extra, at $1,270 and $1,430 respectively.

Bendix/King offers a flatpack stand-alone nav receiver. The **KN 53** features flip-flop frequency management and its dimensions are 1.30" H x 6.31" W x 9.75" D. Price without glideslope: $2,900. With glideslope: $3,816.

The **KY 196A** is the matching comm transceiver. It has 760 channels and flip-flop frequency management, with the addition of memory for the storage of nine frequencies.

Transmitter output of the 28V KY 196A is 16W. The **KY 197A** is a 14V version, with a transmitter output of 7W. Both models are priced at $3,718.

The **KY 96A** is a budget-priced near clone of the KY 196A. The 760-channel set has been given some downscaling that includes an LCD display, plastic trim versus metal, and 5W transmitter power. There is a 14V version, the **KY 97A**, also with 5W output. Both models list for $1,088.

The **KLX 135** combines a VHF transceiver with a GPS receiver, all in one box. For details, see the chapter entitled "A New Breed: GPS/Comms."

Narco

The **Escort II** is a nav/comm that fits into a standard 3⅛" panel hole—and the little round box includes an ECDI. The set has a shared receiver for both the nav and comm functions, so you cannot navigate and communicate simultaneously. A gas discharge display presents all of the information, including frequencies, bearing and course deviation. The ECDI shows light bars radiating to the left or right for VOR and localizer steering. There is no glideslope capability.

The Escort II also has automatic radial centering; by pulling or pressing the OBS knob, you can get a direct bearing to or radial from the VOR station.

Transmitter output: 5W. Price: $2,070.

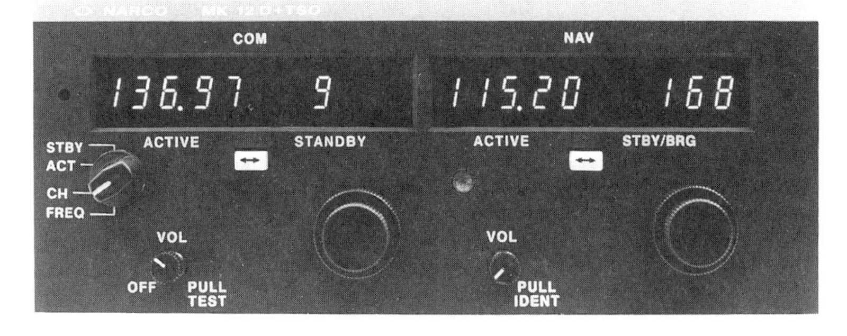

The 12D+ stores 10 comm frequencies and provides a digital readout of the current VOR radial.

The **Mark 12D+** has superseded the Mark 12D. It's a 1 + ½ system nav/comm with built-in audio amplifier, which can be utilized if the installation does not include a separate audio panel. The 12D+ stores 10 comm frequencies and provides a digital readout of the current VOR radial. Transmitter output: 8W. Dimensions: 2.5" H x 6.25" W x 11" D. Price without glideslope: $2,845; with glideslope: $3,324; with glideslope and DME, $4,702. Prices include the appropriate external CDI.

The **NCS 812** offers similar capability to the Mark 12D+ with glideslope and DME, with the addition of a time-to-station (ETE) display and DME hold. Price: $5,287.

The **COM 810+** is a 14V stand-alone comm unit with 760 channels. Its flip-flop system is a little different from other Narco frequency management systems in that frequencies can be entered directly in either the active or standby windows, rather than in the standby window alone. The set has storage for 10 frequencies, a 10W audio amplifier, provisions for multiple audio inputs, and a built-in intercom capability. Transmitter output is 8W. Dimensions: 1.50" H x 6.25" W x 11.0" D. Price: $1,306. The **COM 811+** is a 28V version, priced the same.

Note: The above prices are tied to a one-year warranty. Narco also offers a three-year warranty at a somewhat higher price, which varies from model to model.

Northstar

Northstar's C1 or SmartComm is a remote-mounted transceiver that interfaces with one of their GPS or loran receivers to provide easy access to frequencies of facilities near your plane's present position. For details, see the chapter entitled "A New Breed: GPS/Comms."

Terra

Terra makes a line of radios with the very compact dimensions of 1.6" H x 3.125" W x 11.45" D. Formerly tuned mechanically by means of pushbuttons, the sets now boast gas discharge displays, flip-flop tuning, and storage for 10 frequencies.

The **TX 760 D** is a 760-channel comm set and the **TN 200 D** is the companion nav radio. Note from the dimensions listed above that when they are mounted side by side they take up less space than a typical 1 + ½ nav/comm, but Terra's units are 1 + 1 stand-alones, with no shared components. The **TX 760 D** has a transmitter output of 5W

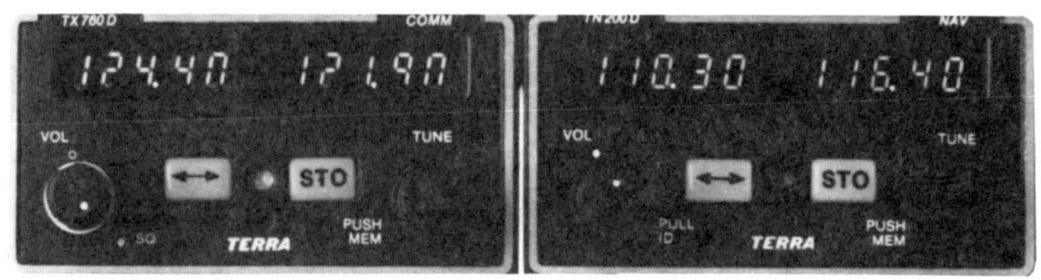

These two compact Terra radios take up less panel space than a single conventional 1 + ½ nav/comm system.

VAL's COM 760 TSO is made by a Salem, Oregon avionics shop. The transceiver is modestly priced at $595.

and lists for $1,090. The TN 200 D is priced at $1,405 with glideslope, $1,140 without.

Terra makes two electronic CDIs: the Tri-Nav ECDI, which works with two nav receivers, and the Tri-Nav C ECDI, which works with one nav receiver and a loran receiver. In either configuration, the ECDI functions as a VOR/LOC/GS indicator. Course deviation is shown in the form of gas discharge bars that radiate from the center. The ECDI features a timer function and automatic radial centering. Each model lists for $985. Terra offers a variety of nav/comm/ECDI packages, including a budget system that utilizes the older mechanical radios.

The **TX 3200** is a stand-alone comm set in the standard mark width that features a gas discharge display, flip-flop tuning, and storage for nine frequencies. Transmitter output is 10W. Dimensions: 1.3" H x 6.25" W x 12.2" D. Price: $1,995.

VAL

VAL Avionics is a radio shop that has gone into the business of marketing its own transceiver—and one with a very modest price tag. The **COM 760 TSO** features a large incandescent display. Frequency management is similar to the ubiquitous flip-flop tuning, but only one frequency is displayed at a time. Programming and transfer of frequencies is done by means of toggle switches.

Transmitter output: 8W. Dimensions: 1.4" H x 6.25" W x 12.5" D. Price: $595.

Icom

The handheld manufacturer has produced an installable comm radio called the **IC-A200 Airband Panel Mount**. The set has an LCD display and memory for nine stored frequencies plus the active and standby frequencies. Transmitter output: 7W. Dimensions: 1.3" H x 6.3" W x 10.7" D. Price: $1,095.

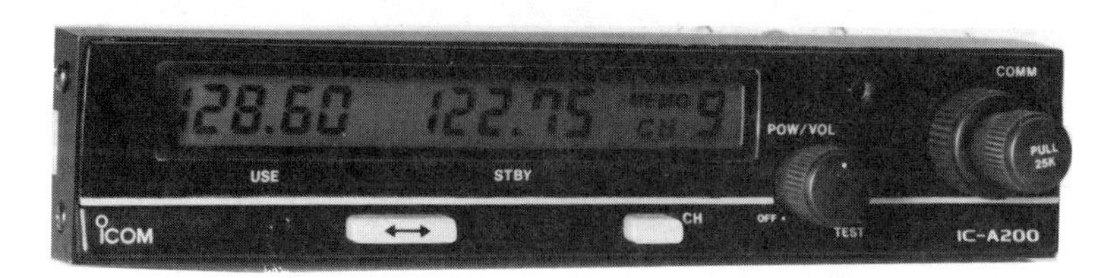

Icom, a company that has made its mark in the handheld field, now offers a panel-mounted transceiver.

TKM

This company makes radios designed as slide-in replacements for some of the older King, Cessna/ARC, and Narco sets. All of the TKM models have LED displays, flip-flop tuning, 760 comm channels, and the interesting ability to store 50 frequencies.

The owner of a King KX 170 or KX 175 can slip his old radio out of its mounting tray and slip in a **TKM MX-170B** without any installation work. The MX-170B supersedes an earlier model, the MX-170, which had a gas discharge display and was more expensive to produce. It will interface with whatever CDI the King unit has been working with.

In the same way, the **MX-300** can be used to replace the ARC RT-308/328 radios, and, with an adapter, some models of the ARC RT-500 series. Then there's the **MX-385**, a replacement of the ARC RT-385, and the MX 12, which replaces the Narco Mark 12. All of these TKM sets list for $1,795.

TKM's MX-300 can provide blessed relief for those who are not thrilled with their ARC radios.

The **MX-300V** has a built-in VOR/LOC ECDI and is provided with mounting hardware for new installations. Dimensions: 2.9" H x 6.25" W x 12" D. Price: $1,895.

The **MX 11 COMM** replaces the Narco COM 11, 11A, 11B, 111, 111B, and 120. It also replaces the COM 10 and 110 when the NAV 10 and NAV 110 are not used in the system. Price: $900.

McCoy

The **MAC 1700** offers another way that owners of older King radios can move into the digital age without giving up their tried-and-true performers. Phil McCoy, a former employee of King, got the idea of adding sophisticated new front ends to the venerable King sets.

This is how it works: You bring your KX 170A, 170B, 175, or 175B to a participating avionics shop. There, the radio's faceplate, electro-mechanical tuning mechanism, and power supply bulkhead will be replaced with a computerized front end. Your set will have an LED display with flip-flop tuning and, in McCoy's standard configuration, 720 comm channels and storage for 10 comm and 10 nav frequencies. There is also a countdown approach timer.

In addition, McCoy offers a menu of three options, and you can choose one, two, or all three. They are as follows:

The "X" option provides 760 comm channels instead of 720.

The "T" option consists of expanded timer functions. One timer can record and recall elapsed flight times for the last eight flights. You can also set in a periodic reminder in half-hour or one-hour increments, say, for switching fuel tanks. Another timer goes up to

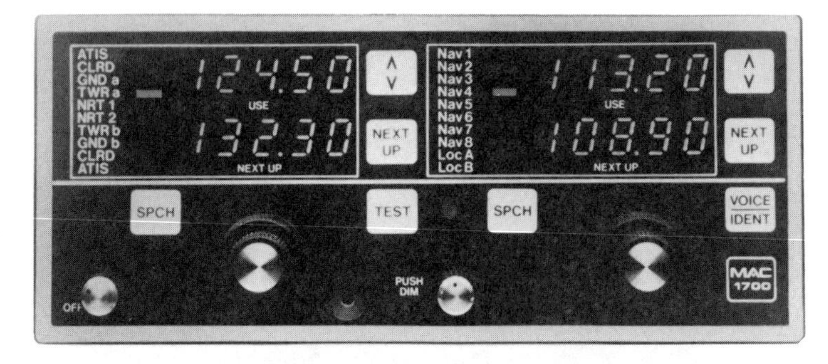

The MAC 1700 brings digital display and frequency storage to the KX 170/175 radios. With the "V" option, it talks to you!

999 hours, good for reminding you of oil changes or other maintenance items based on accumulated time.

The "V" option has a synthesized voice that announces both the active and standby frequencies at the press of a button—an especially desirable feature in the event the display fails. (It can happen with any digital set.) The voice will also keep you advised of the time remaining on the countdown approach timer. In addition, the "V" option has memory for storage of 60 comm and 60 nav frequencies. The price of the modification with any one of the above options is $1,395; with two options, $1,545; with all three options, $1,695. You must choose at least one option; the others can be added later if you wish, at a cost of $150 each.

Note that if you own a KX 170A or 175, it must first be modified with a frequency stability kit at an additional cost of $200. When the radio is further upgraded with one of the front ends mentioned above, it will have 720 channels (or 760 with the "X" option) instead of the original 360 channels.

TEC LINE

S-TEC, the autopilot manufacturer, purchased the Micro Line radios from Collins and is producing these sets under the name TEC LINE. The model designations remain the same.

The TEC LINE nav and comm radios are stand-alone units, most of which have a distinctive square-ish shape; the dimensions are 2.61" H x 3.12" W x 12.45" D.

The **VIR-351** nav receiver has a single incandescent display window that shows either the selected frequency or a digital readout of

The TEC LINE VHF-235's LCD display is gold, rather than the customary silver—perhaps a reflection on the set's original Collins heritage.

the bearing to or radial from the VOR in use. Price: $3,085. The optional remote-mounted GLS-350 glideslope receiver is priced at $1,318.

S-TEC now offers a modernized version of the companion comm transceiver: The **VHF-251A** has 760 channels and stores 10 frequencies; it is a slide-in replacement of the older VHF-250 and 251 models. Transmitter output: 10W. Price: $2,695.

The **VHF-253** comm has a flatpack shape, LCD display, flip-flop frequency management, and memory for four frequencies. A remote frequency transfer button can be installed on the yoke.

Transmitter output: 10W. Dimensions: 1.3" H x 6.3" W x 12.1" D. Price: $3,526. There is no companion nav set.

The IND-350A VOR/LOC indicator and the IND-351A VOR/LOC/GS indicator are priced at $1,318 and $1,465 respectively. Both units have a rectilinear movement.

Integrated Communications Systems

Wag-Aero, the well-known supplier of parts to owners of homebuilt and production aircraft, distributes this multi-featured radio

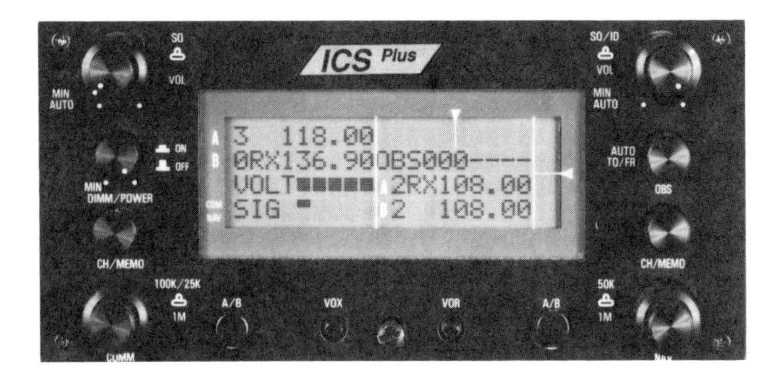

The ICS Plus displays some unique information.

from Japan.

The **ICS Plus** is a nav/comm with 760 comm channels and a built-in glideslope receiver. Also built in is an emergency battery that will power the set for about eight hours of reception or one hour of transmission. The LCD display includes quite a few items: voltage strength, comm and nav signal strength, ECDI with digital bearing, and active and standby frequencies. There is storage for 20 comm and 20 nav frequencies. The set has a built-in intercom with connections for a music system. Transmitter output: 8W. Dimensions: 3" H x 6.25" W x 9.75" D. Price: $1,595.

Radio Systems Technology

Like to build your own? The **RST-572** nav/comm comes in kit form. It has mechanical tuning, via backlit thumbwheels, and a built-in CDI. The nav side has VOR/LOC capability; there is no glideslope receiver. Transmitter output: 2W. Dimensions: 3.5" H x 6.5" W x 10.8" D. The price of $850 includes a mounting tray and connectors, as well as a factory checkout and calibration process. An optional remote ECDI (which will work only with the RST-572) is available for $240; the nav/comm and CDI can be purchased as a package for $1,050.

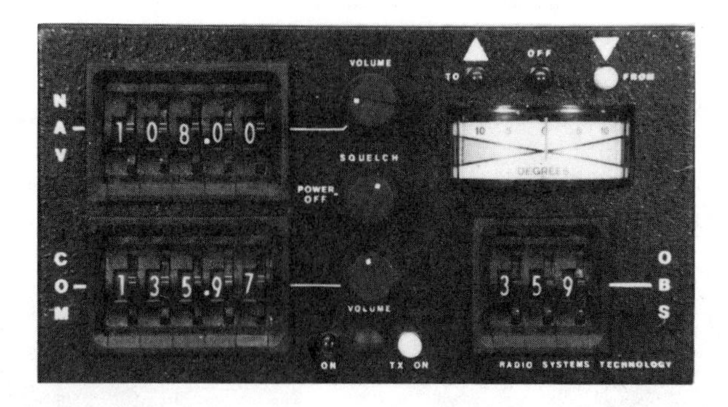

The RST-572 is for do-it-yourselfers. After you've assembled the nav/comm, the factory will calibrate it.

Now let's take a look at an interesting new concept, the GPS/Comm.

15

A New Breed: GPS/Comms

This chapter deals with a relatively new category of black boxes that is sure to grow larger in the future. The traditional nav/comms, as described in the preceding chapter, are VHF transceivers mated with VOR receivers. But more and more pilots are navigating with GPS and don't feel the need to use the VOR system at all. Of course, VOR/LOC/ILS equipment is still essential for IFR approaches—and will continue to be until GPS approaches take over completely—but for many pilots, a system that combines GPS nav with VHF comm can make a lot of sense. This is particularly true when you consider that the computer power that's inherent in a GPS receiver can be used for highly intelligent frequency management.

For this edition of *The GPS, Loran & Nav/Comm Guide,* we have two such models. Common sense tells me that other contenders are being readied for production and might appear at any time. (Probably while this book is being printed—a recurring source of frustration for the author.)

Bendix/King

The KLX 135 is part of the Crown line, which means that you can install it yourself without voiding the warranty. The unit consists of a GPS receiver and VHF comm transceiver combined in one box. The set has an LCD display, with active and standby comm frequencies shown in the upper left hand corner and most of the remaining portion devoted to navigation, airport, flight planning, and calculator pages.

The internal database includes airports, VORs, and NDBs, with a search function for the nine nearest waypoints of each category. Here's a neat way of selecting a comm frequency: One of the airport information pages lists the frequencies for the area. You can use the cursor to select a frequency and with the press of a button enter that frequency in the standby comm slot.

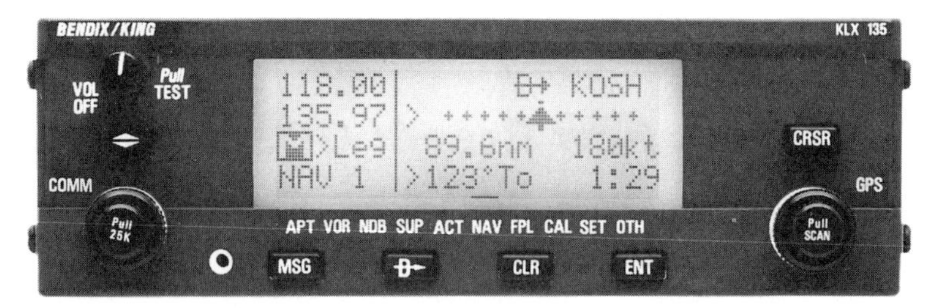

The KLX 135 allows you to select a frequency from an airport information page and place it in the comm standby window.

The set has memory for 250 user waypoints and 10 flight plans of up to 19 legs each. The database can be updated by means of a PC. The comm portion has 760 channels and 5W transmitter power. The comm transceiver is TSOd but the GPS receiver is not, and thus is not IFR certifiable. Price: $3,395.

Northstar

The **SmartComm** is a 760-channel "blind" transceiver that is remotely mounted and utilizes the right-side controls and display of a Northstar 60, 600, or M3 GPS receiver—or an M2 loran set.

Using the position input from the GPS or loran set to which it is connected, the SmartComm gives you a wide selection of frequencies in your area.

Included are the two nearest Approach, Center, ATIS, and Tower frequencies, as well as the five frequencies you used last. There's also a menu of frequencies within 500 nm of your present position; these are selectable by category, such as Center, FSS, etc.

The system will require an upgrade of existing GPS and loran sets, to accommodate the necessary volume control; new production units will have the mod. Transmitter output is 5W. Price: $1,995.

Now let's look at the more familiar type of handheld—the VHF transceiver.

16

VHF Handhelds

The type of handhelds we are discussing are battery-powered transceivers that cover the standard aircraft communications band. All of the sets listed in this chapter will also receive voice communications on the VOR nav channels—and some models can display steering information as well.

Advantages

Handhelds have become very popular because they can be used in a variety of ways. Here are some examples:

Primary radio. A handheld can function as the sole means of communication (and, in some cases, navigation) in an aircraft without an electrical system, such as an ultralight, sailplane, balloon or simple homebuilt.

Emergency radio. If your aircraft's electrical system fails, the handheld will provide a backup radio. This safety function is especially important for IFR pilots. You or your radio shop can install a BNC connector to your plane's comm antenna, which will give you considerably more range than the "rubber duck" antenna that is customarily provided for the handheld. If your handheld provides nav guidance, you will need a connection to the aircraft's nav antenna for optimum accuracy.

In the event of a plane crash that disables the aircraft's radios, a handheld can be used to summon aid and provide directions to the rescuers.

Clearance convenience. No longer need you wait for and copy an IFR clearance with the plane's engine chugging away or the battery draining. Call for your clearance in the pilot's lounge, via the handheld.

Weather update. When you're waiting out the weather at home—or worse yet, in a motel room—you can get a good idea of local conditions by tuning in the ATIS or monitoring the transmissions of pilots and controllers.

A handheld can also be used as a mobile base station for coordinating aircraft during a fly-in, ground crew for sailplanes or hot air balloons, skydiving instruction, etc. Be aware that the FCC requires you to have a Ground Station Authorization (Application Form 406) for transmissions on the ground, as well as an Aircraft Radio Station License (Application Form 404) for aircraft use.

Considerations

Here are some of the criteria you'll find useful when selecting a handheld:

Navigation capability. While all of the handhelds listed can receive voice communications on the 200 nav channels, some models also process the VOR signals and provide steering information by means of a built-in ECDI and/or a digital radial/bearing display.

Frequency management. Some handhelds are mechanically tuned by thumbwheels, while others are electronically tuned by pushbuttons and can store up to 10 frequencies, as well as scan through the frequencies. These functions are useful, but they are more complicated to operate; therefore, if you plan to use this type of set as backup equipment, review its operation from time to time, so you won't have added pressure during an emergency.

Power source. Most handhelds use a rechargeable NiCad (nickel-cadmium) battery pack as their standard power source. It is important to note that a NiCad pack can lose its charge within a matter of weeks, so it's up to you to charge it regularly or you may find that it's dead when you need it.

Some sets are designed with a battery case that twists or slides from the body of the unit for easy replacement. This is especially handy if a spare case containing standard AA alkaline batteries is available; although alkaline batteries cannot be recharged, they normally have a shelf life of a year or more, and thus are a good backup for the NiCad pack.

High/low power settings. Several units have high and low transmit power settings, giving you the choice of maximum range or minimum battery drain.

Construction. Some sets have cases made of plastic, while others are constructed of metal. While the plastic cases are generally quite durable, the metal cases are more likely to withstand an accidental free fall from baggage compartment to tarmac, and they may also be more effective at heat dissipation.

Accessories. Handhelds usually come with an ear plug and a battery charging unit for 115V house current or a 12V car, plane or boat system. The range of optional accessories varies by manufacturer.

Some companies offer a rapid charger that charges the NiCad pack in an hour, as opposed to the 5 to 18 hours required by standard chargers. As mentioned earlier, an alkaline battery case, or a spare NiCad case, is good to have as a backup.

A remote speaker/mike is useful—or better yet, a method of connecting the handheld to a headset, either directly or through a patch cord. Remember, a handheld that sounds loud and clear at home may be practically inaudible in a noisy airplane.

The Models

Here are product descriptions of handhelds that are currently available, listed by manufacturer. Note that the transmit power of a given model may be specified as CW (carrier wave), PEP (peak envelope power) or both. While it is traditional for the manufacturers of panel-mounted nav/comms to list their transmitter power as CW, some of the handheld manufacturers use the PEP measurement. Depending on transmitter efficiency, PEP will tend to be somewhere around three times the value of CW; thus, an output of 2W CW is roughly equivalent to an output of 6W PEP.

Like the panel-mounted comm sets, the more recent handhelds are designed with 760-channel capability, to utilize 40 new channels that are being allocated gradually for ATIS, AWOS, ATC, and unicom communications. I have noted 760 channels where applicable; the other models have 720 channels. As mentioned earlier, all of the handhelds can receive the nav channels, and some provide VOR steering information in addition to voice.

Icom

The **IC-A20** has keyboard tuning and a built-in ECDI as well as a digital readout of the bearing to or the radial from the VOR in use. There are 16 memory channels and three scanning functions, including a memory lockout scan. Other features include semi-duplex operation and instant access to 121.5 MHz. Transmit power: 5W PEP. Dimensions: 7.8" H x 2.56" W x 1.38" D. Weight: 1.47 lb. Case: Plastic and metal. Price: $625. The **IC-A2** is similar to the IC-A20; the major difference is that it does not have the navigation features. Price: $525.

The **IC-A21** is a step-up version of the IC-A20. Among its extra features is a tuning control knob, which can be used instead of the set's keyboard to speed up the frequency selection process. The unit has 760 comm channels and also receives the National Weather Service channels. These broadcasts are not specific to aviation, but they include local temperatures, approximate surface winds (west, northeast, etc.), general sky conditions, and other useful information. There is storage capacity for 20 frequencies. Price: $660.

Bendix/King

The **KX 99** has 760 comm channels. Its displays include an ECDI and a digital TO/FROM bearing readout. An Auto Course mode automatically centers the CDI on a TO or FROM indication. The unit can receive the National Weather Service channels.

The set's side-tone feature enables you to hear your own voice transmissions. Programming is by keyboard, with 10 memory channels and scanning capability. A headphone/mike adapter is a standard accessory. Optional acccssories include an

The KX 99 can receive the National Weather Service channels.

alkaline battery case and adapters that allow the set to be connected to the aircraft's comm and nav antennas.

Transmit power: 1.5W CW. Dimensions: 8" H x 2.6" W x 1.6" D. Weight: 1 lb, 12 oz. Case: Plastic. Price: $595.

An optional tray allows the TR-720 to be used as a panel-mounted transceiver.

Communications Specialists

The **TR-720** has mechanical thumbwheel tuning and memory for storage of three frequencies. A half-duplex function allows the user to transmit on the comm band while monitoring a VOR frequency, which may be necessary when communicating with a Flight Service Station.

The manufacturer offers a wide variety of optional accessories, including an alkaline battery case, 750 ma NiCad pack (a 450 ma NiCad pack is standard), 10W power amplifier, remote speaker mike, headset, adapter for standard mike or headset, and several types of battery chargers.

Transmit power: 1W nominal, 3W PEP. Dimensions: 6.6" H x 2.6" W x 1.5" D. Weight: 1.2 lb. Case: Plastic. Price: $632.

The TR-720 can be mounted in a 3⅛" instrument panel hole by means of a tray made and marketed by Ken Brock Mfg. When the handheld is in the panel, its NiCad pack is maintained in a state of charge by the aircraft's electrical system, so it is always available as either a primary or standby comm radio. The unit can be removed easily for use as a portable. Price of the tray: $195.

Sporty's Pilot Shop

This popular pilot supply company markets their own handheld. The **A300** has 760 comm channels and features a TO/FROM bearing display, but no ECDI. Features include keyboard tuning, 20 programmable frequencies, scanning, and half-duplex operation. Sporty's flies in the face of tradition by providing an alkaline battery case as standard (batteries not included) and a NiCad pack as an option at $75. Transmit power: 1.5W CW. Dimensions: 6.75" H x 2.5" W x 1.5" D. Weight: 1 lb, 1.3 oz. Case: Plastic. Price: $365.

Terra

The **TPX 720** has mechanical thumbwheel tuning; there is no memory for frequency storage. Mike and headphone jacks are standard aircraft size, in contrast with most other handhelds that have small jacks. The set has high/low power settings. Power is provided by an internal case containing 10 standard AA NiCad batteries; access requires a Phillips screwdriver. Optional accessories include telescopic antenna, headset, mike, and push-to-talk switch.

Transmit power: High—2.5W CW, 8W PEP; low—.5W CW, 2W PEP. Dimensions: 9.5" H x 3.27" W x 1.9" D. Weight: 2.1 lb. Case: Metal. Price: $595.

Handhelds don't need to be installed in an airplane, but most other radios do. So let's spend the next few pages discussing how to find the right people to do your installation and service work.

17

How to Choose a Radio Shop

You should take as much care to get the right installation as you take to get the right equipment. And that means, for one thing, finding a first-rate avionics shop. And even after you've found a good shop, there are procedures you can follow to help assure that the installation will be tailored to your needs.

In this chapter, I'll offer some suggestions on finding and evaluating a shop, matters to discuss before the installation, items to check after the installation, and things you can do to prolong the life of your avionics.

Considerations

Quality of the installation. Most of us don't get to see the "hidden values" of an installation, because they are indeed well hidden behind panels, bulkheads, etc. A good installation includes high-quality connectors and adequate lengths of the best wiring, properly secured for a long, trouble-free life. Care is taken in antenna placement, and the antenna is well bonded to the aircraft skin and secured with a doubler if necessary. Panel cutouts are neat and precise. The plane is returned to you with the interior as clean as the way you left it, and no missing screws. The installer does his job with competence and pride.

Scheduling. The chances are you don't want to tie up your plane any longer than necessary, so ideally the work will start on the scheduled day and will be finished on a date that's *reasonably* close to that which was estimated. Don't expect miracles in this respect; there may be some unforeseen problems lurking in the bowels of your plane, especially if the shop has not worked on it before. Also, your job may get bumped a bit if a customer limps in with an emergency. However, a good shop will be sufficiently organized and disciplined that you won't be getting a series of excuses and broken promises.

Cost. Some time ago, I asked several shops to bid on installing a piece of equipment in my plane. Three bids came in at $1,600 for the labor. Then there was another bid at $800, and yet another at "$2,500 to $3,000." That last bid impressed me on several counts, one of which was the offhanded manner in which the manager allowed himself $500 worth of leeway.

The substantial difference between the high and low bids did not surprise me. It has been my experience over the years that estimates on a given job can range quite widely. For one thing, shops differ in the way they price their jobs. Some have a policy of charging list price for the equipment and installing it at no extra charge. Other shops discount the equipment and charge for the installation. Of course, what you want to know is how much the total cost is going to be, regardless of how it's arrived at.

To make sure you're comparing apples to apples, ask each shop to provide as much detail as possible on the materials they will be supplying, as well as their installation warranty and any other factors they feel are worth considering.

One such factor may be a trade-in allowance on any equipment you'll be replacing. Get the shop's bid before you talk about a trade-in, otherwise they may be tempted to build the allowance into the price of the job. The trade-in you are offered will depend on the shop's policy regarding used equipment. Some shops won't handle trade-ins, period. Of those that will, some repair and resell the old boxes; others wholesale what they can and trash the rest, or keep them around for spare parts. Incidentally, many shop owners have told me that the average customer has an exaggerated idea of the value of his old radios. If you insist on getting a higher trade-in than the shop thinks the equipment is worth, they may give it to you but they'll find a way to make it up in the installation.

Installation warranty. The manufacturer's warranty that comes with your radio covers the cost of fixing (within the period of the warranty) whatever goes wrong with the box itself; it does not cover installation glitches. Each shop has its own policy on handling installation problems, generally not in writing, and often vaguely worded, such as, "We stand behind our work." (How far behind?) Some shops are more specific, offering to guarantee their installation for a time equal to the manufacturer's warranty, or for the life of the plane, or, as I once heard it expressed, "For your lifetime or mine, whichever comes first."

Bear in mind that your airplane is a traveling machine, and if a radio poops out when you're a thousand miles from home, any authorized dealer for that brand should honor the manufacturer's warranty, because he knows the factory will pay his bill. An installation problem is something else, and the best way to handle that situation is to ask the dealer to phone the shop that did the installation and work things out.

Looking for Mr. Goodwire

Finding the right shop can take a bit of research. Ask other aircraft owners for recommendations, particularly those who fly with the kind of radios you're interested in. (That way, you'll find out something about the radios as well as the installation.) If your local FBO doesn't have his own shop, ask whom he uses; it stands to reason he can't afford to do business with a shop whose poor work results in downtime on his rental fleet. Get the name of the local field rep of the manufacturer whose products you're interested in, and ask him for referrals. He's not likely to knock any of his dealers, but he'll probably steer you to the better ones.

When you find a shop that interests you, ask to speak to someone in authority—preferably the owner or manager. If you're still undecided about which radios to buy and want his advice, give him some clues: tell him what kind of plane you have, what kind of flying you do, and what kind of budget you have in mind.

Whoever deals with you should be knowledgeable about the equipment, not only in technical terms, but in operational terms—that is, he should be able to communicate what it will do for you as a pilot. If you're looking for a loran or GPS, see if any models are lit up on the display case and ask for a demonstration. (Some shop owners can also give demos in their own aircraft.) During the demonstration, you'll learn not only about the capabilities of the equipment, but you'll also get an idea of how much the shop representative knows about the product.

If he recommends a particular unit, ask why. Often you'll get the answer, "Oh, we sell a lot of them and they don't come back for repairs." That may be the perfect set from a technician's point of view, but I would want to know more about what it will do for me as a pilot.

Try to inspect at least one of their installations—for the neatness of their work, if nothing else.

Ask for names and phone numbers of customers, preferably those who own your type of airplane, and call them later on. (Don't worry about bothering strangers; most pilots love to talk about their airplanes and equipment.)

If you decide to try a shop out on a repair job, you'll want to know the basis for their charges. Some shops will offer a flat rate, but most charge "time and materials." Before you blow a fuse at their prices, bear in mind that the better shops have a substantial investment in test equipment and pay good wages for qualified technicians.

Get it in Writing

Even if the shop is charging by the hour, ask for a written estimate. I must confess that I had an unhappy experience awhile back when my entire avionics panel was redone. The project, which stretched into four months, was handled by a shop that had been doing all my radio work for years, and we had a good relationship. This lulled me into forgetting to follow my own advice. When I got the bill I was stunned. If I had maintained better communication with the shop (and vice versa), I probably would have made some other choices along the way.

That having been said, here's some more advice.

Ask about a warranty on repairs as well as installations. Some shops will not warranty repair work on old equipment because it may not keep up to specs for very long. In this case, the manager may try to talk you into upgrading to new radios, and he may very well be right.

You might want to give some brownie points to a shop that's a member of the Aircraft Electronics Association. The AEA was founded in 1957, primarily to get shop owners to talk to each other (they used to feud something awful), as well as communicate better with the manufacturers and generally improve their standards. At this writing, there are approximately a thousand members worldwide. Through training programs and national and regional conventions, members exchange information about equipment, techniques, and ways of improving customer service while maintaining a sound businesslike operation. I've attended their conventions for more than a decade, and each time I have come away impressed.

Before and After

Before work commences on your installation, discuss it thoroughly with the shop person responsible for the job. Make sure you are in agreement as to where the radios, instruments, and switches will be placed. If you expect to be adding specific radios in the future, consider having the wiring put in place while the panel and interior are opened up. You might also have the shop check the old wiring and replace whatever looks as if it might cause trouble.

Be sure that there will be adequate provisions for cooling the avionics; more on that essential point shortly.

If the owner's manual is available, take it home and bone up on the operation of your new equipment while the installation is in progress. This is especially important if you're buying a loran or GPS receiver; even the simplest of those units requires study.

When you pick up the plane after the work is completed, take plenty of time to assure yourself that everything is the way it should be. Check to see that everything in the panel—not just the new gear—is functioning properly; who knows what connections may have been dislodged? Try it out in the air as well as on the ramp. If you have any questions, now's the best time to raise them.

Ask for a wiring diagram of the installation and keep it in the plane; this can reduce exploration time if another shop has to work on it. Make certain all of the paperwork has been completed and signed off as necessary.

Radios by Mail—a Good Idea?

Page through the aviation newspapers and you'll see some very attractive looking bargains advertised by avionics mail order companies. Does it make sense to order a radio by mail? Maybe—but be aware that in some cases the savings could be illusory.

For example, there's a mail order company that runs huge ads in *TRADE-A-PLANE* comparing manufacturers' list prices with their own lower "sale" prices. The only trouble is, some of the so-called "list prices" they display are out of date and are actually higher than the latest list prices (yes, manufacturers actually *lower* their list prices occasionally—sometimes to "keep down" with the competition, sometimes to clear out a model that's not selling well), and this outfit's "sale" prices are within a few dollars of the *real* list prices.

This same mail order firm offers discontinued models and even *overhauled* units without bothering to identify them as such.

While it is possible that the company also advertises legitimate deals, I would not feel comfortable buying from an outfit that conducts business in this manner.

And they are not alone; there are other mail order firms that use these and other dubious tactics. Here's another example: Often an avionics manufacturer will offer its dealers a package deal on two products that complement each other, such as a nav/comm and a CDI. Because of the pricing structure, the manufacturer is virtually giving away the CDI. Some sellers will pass the package savings along to the customer, while others will retail the units separately.

I'm not saying that all mail order vendors are tricksters, but if you see an ad for a great avionics bargain, you would be well advised to ask some pointed questions to help ensure that you are being offered what you really want.

Assuming you find a genuinely good buy, there's the matter of getting your bargain box installed in the plane (unless, of course, it's a portable). Walk into an avionics shop with a mail order radio under your arm and one of two things is likely to happen. 1) They'll throw you out. 2) They'll install it at top rates, probably wiping out whatever saving you thought you were making. Under Scenario #2, if the radio doesn't work, they'll shrug. The box may or may not be protected by a manufacturer's warranty. If it's warranteed by the mail order merchandiser, you'll have to ship the set back to them.

My suggestion is to find a good avionics shop and establish a happy relationship there. Realize that the shop expects to make a reasonable profit on equipment sales, installation and service. In return, you should expect good advice, quality workmanship, and an expeditious solution to any problems that arise. It's a two-way street.

Keeping Your Avionics Healthy

Awhile back, I called some people I know at various avionics manufacturers and asked for their best suggestions on keeping radios out of the shop. The first thing each one of these gentlemen said was, "Give them proper cooling." It's true: heat is the radio's worst enemy, but you can combat the foe in several ways.

A cooling fan is a wise investment; in fact, some manufacturers require forced air cooling of certain radios to keep the warranty in force. Ram air cooling is less satisfactory than a fan, because it can bring moisture from the outside air into the radios.

On a hot day, temperatures can build up in the cockpit that far exceed the TSO specifications of the radios, so if you store your plane outside, invest in a canopy cover or a set of thermal screens. Also, keep the doors and windows open while you're taxiing and turn on just one comm until the heat is dissipated.

Another manufacturer's thought on keeping your avionics healthy is to run them all whenever you fly; it's a fallacy to try to prolong the life of your radios by keeping them off when you're not using them. (An exception is a weather radar utilizing a magnetron, because that component has a specific life span.)

If your plane is not equipped with an avionics master switch, consider installing one—or better yet, *two*—to prevent your accidentally having a radio on when you fire up the engine. This can cause problems, because the starter motor is a big inductor, and when it's turning it draws a lot of current over a short period of time; that can induce a voltage spike.

Why *two* avionics masters? Redundancy. I had one switch fail while I was flying through the busy Los Angeles basin, and all the lights on the panel went out. It was nice to be able to flip the backup switch and see them all come on again.

This is the last chapter of *The GPS, Loran & Nav/Comm Guide.* But don't stop here. There is a considerable amount of additional information waiting for you in the Appendices.

Appendix A

Understanding Latitude & Longitude

Just as you've learned to think in terms of radial and distance when you are navigating with VOR equipment, so should you learn to think in terms of latitude and longitude when navigating with a loran or GPS receiver.

True, GPS and loran sets with their sophisticated computers require far less pilot input than a VOR receiver, but you should resist the temptation to dope off and let the radio become captain as well as navigator. Both loran and GPS, while extremely accurate, are subject to a variety of anomalies, and at times the set may stop providing information—or, worse yet, give out incorrect data.

Also, a familiarity with lat/lon will give you a method of determining your position along your track. And it will help prevent mistakes when you're programming the coordinates of a waypoint.

So let's review the geographic coordinate system, which is the foundation for loran and GPS navigation.

Lines of longitude (also known as meridians) run north and south, connecting the North Pole and the South Pole. They are numbered in angular degrees—from 0° to 180° east and west of the prime meridian, which runs through Greenwich, England. Each line of longitude forms a great circle; that is, it outlines a plane that cuts through the center of the earth. Therefore, all lines of longitude are roughly the same length. If you were to cut an orange lengthwise into even slices, your knife would cut along the equivalent of lines of longitude. (See Fig. A-1.)

Lines of latitude (also called parallels) run east and west, parallel to each other. They, too, are numbered in angular degrees, from 0° to 90° north and south of the equator. Only the equator forms a latitudinal great circle, the other lines of latitude becoming smaller as they get closer to the poles. (See Fig. A-2.)

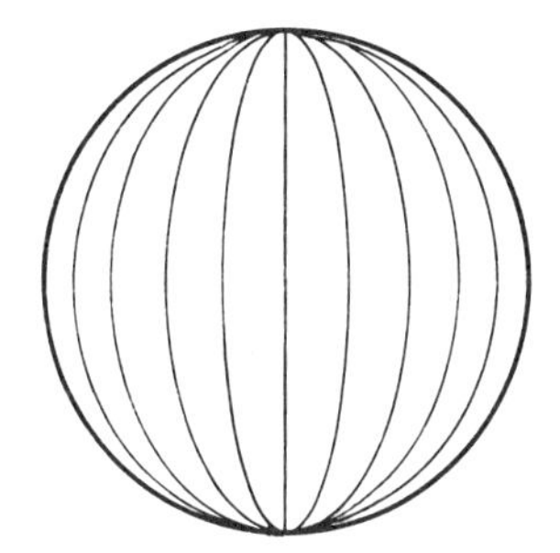

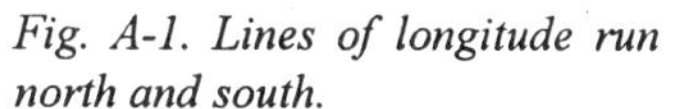

Fig. A-1. Lines of longitude run north and south.

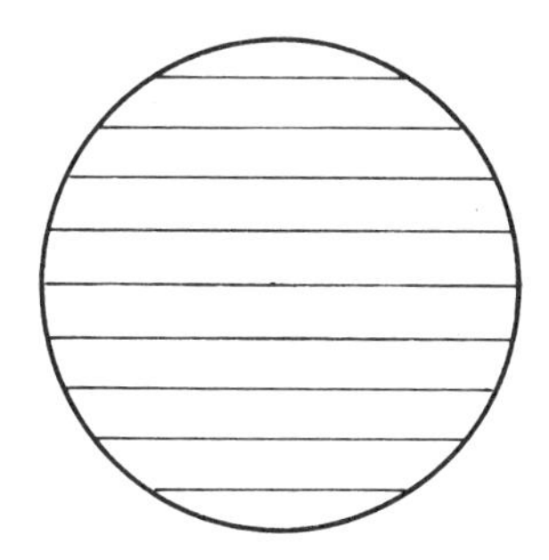

Fig. A-2. Lines of latitude run east and west

Each degree is divided into 60 arc minutes, and each minute is divided into 60 arc seconds.

You can determine the lat/lon coordinates of your present position or of a waypoint with the aid of the parallels and meridians that are drawn on the WAC, sectional and terminal area charts prepared by the National Ocean Service.

The WAC charts have their lines of latitude and longitude spaced 1° apart, with incremental hatchmarks indicating each of the 60 minutes between degrees. (For ease of reference, the hatchmarks are drawn progressively larger at the one, five, 10 and 30 minute intervals.)

The sectional charts can be used in the same way. The major difference is that the lines of longitude and latitude are drawn at intervals of ½°, or 30 minutes, rather than at intervals of 1°. On the terminal area charts, lines appear every ¼° , or 15 minutes.

As an example, if you use a sectional chart to determine the lat/lon position of Banning Municipal Airport, you will see that the field is located approximately five increments south of the 34 latitude line and about nine increments east of the 117 longitude line. Its precise address is 3355'23"N, 11650'59"W.

However, instead of using the traditional degrees, minutes, and seconds, the loran computer thinks in terms of degrees, minutes, and hundredths of a minute. Thus, as you pass over Banning, the nav display will show something like 33-55.38N and 116-50.98W. (See Fig. A-3.)

To convert seconds into hundredths of a minute, divide the seconds by 60.

Since a degree of latitude represents about 60 nm, you can use the chart's vertical hatchmarks as a scale for measuring distance, with each small increment equaling about 1 nm.

However, you cannot use this trick with the hatchmarks that run horizontally between the lines of longitude, unless you happen to be situated at the equator—for it is only at the earth's midsection that a minute of longitude equals a nautical mile. Remember the orange

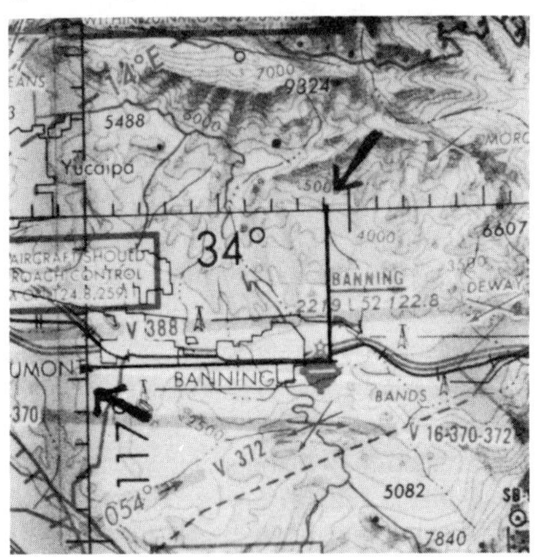

Fig. A-3 Use care in determining lat/lon coordinates from a chart.

slices; the lines of longitude converge as they move toward the poles. (They appear to be parallel on your chart, but they aren't.)

Although you probably won't be constantly verifying your lat/lon position during a cross-country flight, it's a good idea to make a note of the coordinates at your points of departure and destination, and possibly at a mid-point. This will help you to monitor your receiver's performance.

To remember which way the numbers should be changing along your route of flight, think of the memory jogger *east is least and west is best;* it works as well for longitude as it does for compass variation. That is, the longitude will decrease as you move in an easterly direction, and will increase as you go west.

And if you think of north as *up* and south as *down,* you'll find it easy to remember how the latitude numbers go. (These rules do not apply everywhere, but they work on the North American Continent.)

It wouldn't hurt to practice lat/lon navigation every so often by using your chart to determine the coordinates of various waypoints. That way, you'll maintain fluency in the language of GPS and loran.

Appendix B

A Guide to Guides

Here's a small collection of guides that I recommend. They will be especially beneficial to those who navigate with loran or GPS, because they contain the lat/lons of airports and navaids, along with their three-letter IDs. Moreover, these publications will prove useful to *any* pilot who flies to unfamiliar places. Most of them list what I will call *airport facilities*, which includes the airport name and ID, city, elevation, runway lengths and surfaces, lighting, and fuel availability. And many of the guides go on to provide what I will call *traveler's tips*, which refers to ground transportation, food, lodging, places of interest, etc.

A few of the guides get extra brownie points for having a cross-reference section, so you can find Pine Mountain Lake Airport without having to know it's located in Groveland.

AC-U-KWIK Airport/FBO Directory is 4" x 6" with plasticized cover, listing airports in the US and Canada with over 3000 feet of paved runway. Shows lat/lon, airport facilities, related navaids, frequencies/radial/distance from VORs, and phones for FSS, AWOS, ATIS, and FBOs. Airports and navaids are cross-referenced. Toll-free numbers for major hotels and car rentals are listed. Revised annually. Published by Intertec Publishing, P.O.B. 12901, Overland Park, KS 66282; 800-654-6776.

Aviator's Data Log, a 3" x 5" paperback, lists lat/lon, airport facilities, and FSS phones for public use airports, private airports with hard-surface runways, seaplane bases and military fields in the 50 states, Puerto Rico and the Virgin Islands. VORs and NDBs are covered in the 50 states, Canada, the Caribbean and Central America; the VORs are cross-referenced. Also included are outer markers, runways coordinates and FSS phones. Revised periodically. Published by Aviator's Data Log, 1210 Georgia Street, Louisiana, MO 63353; 314-754-3197.

National Ocean Survey Airport/Facility Directory comes in seven paperbound 5" x 8" volumes that together cover the lower 48 states, Puerto Rico and the Virgin Islands. Heliports and seaplane bases are included. Lists lat/lon, airport facilities, cautions, FSS phones, TPA (traffic pattern altitude), and distance to the city. Also included are FSDO phones and addresses, VOR receiver check points and VOTs, operational limitations of VOR/VORTAC/TACAN stations, and frequencies for ARTCCs (Air Route Traffic Control Centers). Revised every 56 days. Order from NOAA Distribution Branch, N/CG33, National Ocean Service, Riverdale, MD 20737

AOPA'S Aviation USA is a paper-bound 8½" x 11" book that covers the USA and possessions, and lists lat/lon, airport facilities, diagrams of airports with instrument approach procedures, TPA, cautions, FBO phones, fees. Also included are FAA phone numbers, selected FARs, traveler's tips, nearby tourist attractions, type of aircraft storage, airline or air taxi service, and even a directory of aviation businesses. Revised annually, and included with AOPA membership. Published by Aircraft Owners and Pilots Association (AOPA), 421 Aviation Way, Frederick, MD 21701.

Flight Guide is published in three leatherette ring binders, each about 5" x 5", covering the Eastern, Central and Western portions of the lower 48 states. Includes lat/lon, airport facilities, cautions, FSS phone, TPA, VORs, FBO phones and fees, and traveler's tips. Most airports are diagrammed, with area maps showing local landmarks for many locations. Airports are cross-referenced. TCAs and ARSAs are diagrammed. Standard broadcast stations within 30 miles of airports are listed. Even the dividers have been stuffed with such information as VHF reception distances, airway use rules, an ISA chart, altimeter setting procedures, etc. Published by Airguide Publications, Inc., 1207 Pine Avenue, PO Box 1288, Long Beach, CA 90801.

JeppGuide (formerly TannGuide) covers the lower 48 states in seven three-ring, loose-leaf, vinyl-covered binders measuring 7" x 9". Gives lat/lons, airport diagrams, frequencies, obstructions, distances and radials from four VORs, FBO services, location of phones on the field, lodging, restaurants, and car rentals. A unique "yellow pages" section shows, alphabetically by state, every airport at which you'll find such useful services as 24-hr emergency repairs, 24-hr refueling, avionics repairs, oxygen, paint shops, used aircraft sales, etc. Updates are published every 120 days, and three come free with purchase. Published by Jeppesen, 55 Inverness Dr. East, Englewood, CO 80112; 800-621-5377.

GPS-Loran Navigation Atlas is 11" x 11" spiral bound and contains 26 Skyprints charts and 26 GPS charts. Included are the lat/lons of airports, VORs, off-airport NDBs, and intersections, as well as enroute and airport frequencies. There's also an airport and VOR identifier decoder. Published by Air Chart System; 13368 Beach Avenue, Venice, CA 90292; 310-822-1996.

Pilot's Guide to California Airports is encased in a sturdy vinyl-bound ring binder, 7" x 9". Information includes lat/lon, airport facilities, cautions, FSS and FBO phones, TPA, and VORs. Controlled airports are depicted with aerial photos, diagrams and fold-out maps with VFR reporting points, so when you're told to "report the Mormon Temple," you'll know what it looks like. For uncontrolled airports, diagrams and nearby landmarks are shown. Traveler's tips, noteworthy local restaurants, and spots of interest are mentioned, plus phone numbers for hotels and car rental agencies. Revisions four times a year. Published by Optima Publications, 180 Second Street, Los Altos, CA 94022; 415-941-4333.

Pilot's Guide to Southwestern Airports has the same format as the *Pilot's Guide to California Airports,* listing airports in Arizona, Colorado, Utah, Nevada, and New Mexico. Revisions three times a year. Published by RGR Publications, PO Box 926, Penn Valley, CA 95946; 916-432-3689.

Airports of Baja California and Central America comes in a 6" x 9" ring binder. Author Arnold Senterfitt has been visiting, measuring, and evaluating south-of-the-border landing strips for more than 20 years. The book is a gold mine of tips and includes just about everything: lat/lons, airport facilities, population of the nearest town, FSS frequencies when available, VORs, photos and diagrams of airports and landing strips, charts, cautions, fees, tiedown and maintenance availability, camping, etc. There are hints on getting through customs, insurance requirements, finding fuel, food and water. There is even a small section with Spanish phrases and phonetic pronunciations for place names. Senterfitt also offers an aviation chart of Mexico. Published by Arnold Senterfitt's New Baja Bush Pilots, PO Box 34280, San Diego, CA 92163; 619-297-5587.

Appendix C

GPS & Loran Antenna Installation

This appendix will be of especial interest to homebuilders, as well as others who are qualified to do their own installations.

GPS Antennas

The following section on GPS antennas was prepared by John Stites of Comant Industries, a leading antenna manufacturer.

Since GPS signals are line-of-sight and do not pass through metal, a GPS external antenna should be placed on top of the aircraft, near the centerline and away from protuberances that could shade the antenna and thus prevent a full-sky view of the GPS constellation.

Several different types of antennas are in use today. In some cases, a Low Noise Amplifier (LNA) is included to boost the strength of these relatively weak signals and to make up for coaxial cable losses between the antenna and the receiver. For some applications, RF Filtering in the LNA circuit is required to reduce interference of out of band signals (see *Filtering,* below). Power for the LNA is provided by the GPS receiver via the coaxial cable center conductor. Antennas with an LNA are referred to as *active,* while those without an LNA are called *passive.*

The types of antenna elements you'll find in most use today are: quadrifilar, microstrip patch, and crossed slot.

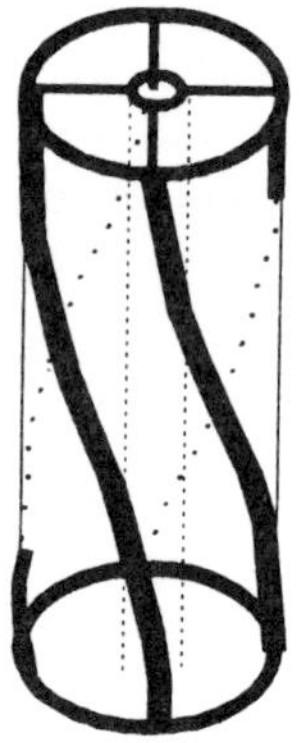

Quadrifilar

The quadrifilar *(right)* is a multi-arm helix using phase shifters to produce the circular polarization. It is considered to be the "balanced" type, requiring no ground plane; therefore, it is particularly suitable for handheld GPS receivers.

This antenna element is typically 3 to 4 inches long and 1 inch in diameter.

Microstrip Patch

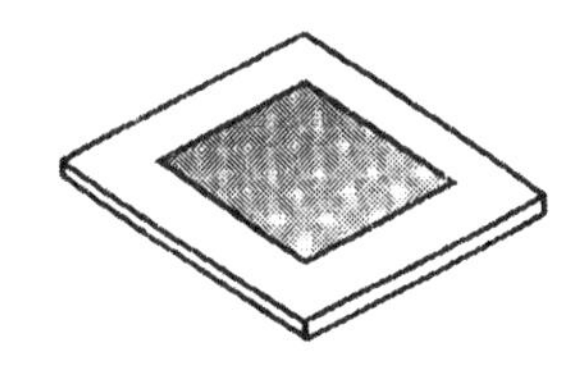

The microstrip patch is much like an RF capacitor in that a small ceramic wafer is imprinted with a radiator on one side and a ground plane on the other. The size of the radiator is critical in determining the desired narrow-band frequency of 1575 MHz. The location of the feed point is critical in determining the polarization, impedance, and axial ratio. These antenna elements are typically 1½ to 2 inches square and about 0.1 inch thick. Different dielectric substrates of various thickness allow the use of a smaller radiator and overall smaller antenna. The more frequency-stable units utilize the Alumina-Ceramic substrate, which is white in color.

Crossed-Slot

The crossed-slot is a low profile antenna that is about the same size as the microstrip patch. However, because it is a broader-bandwidth device, the overall gain is more difficult to achieve with this antenna.

Comparing All Three

The quadrifilar reportedly gives better low angle (on the horizon) gain, but is a higher profile antenna than the others, relegating it to applications where aerodynamic drag is not a serious factor. The microstrip patch is probably the least expensive to produce and exhibits very good gain at the zenith and acceptable gain on the horizon. Although slot-type antennas are more difficult to design, fabrication tolerances are not as critical as with the microstrip patch antenna.

All of these types exhibit roughly +3 to +5 dBi maximum gain.

Remote Antennas

Handheld GPS receivers generally come with a standard or optional antenna that can be remotely mounted near a windshield or window area, usually by means of a suction cup. Some remotes have an internal LNA to overcome coaxial cable losses and to increase the level of the received signals before they arrive at the receiver.

An inside location does not always allow the antenna to receive the maximum number of available satellites, especially when the aircraft changes attitude. This deficiency is correctable by installing an external antenna. In some cases, these are available from the GPS receiver manufacturer. Kits with all of the required hardware, including coaxial cable, connectors, and adapters can also be obtained from Comant Industries. These kits are available for most current GPS receivers, with antennas approved under TSO C129.

Filtering

GPS receivers, like other RF receivers, are susceptible to interfering signals. These originate from other equipment on the aircraft that transmit RF energy. Interference that occurs in the same frequency band as the GPS signals cannot be filtered out, but the antenna can be placed a greater distance from the source antenna to reduce the coupling of the interfering signal.

For out of band interfering signals, of which there are many on both aircraft and ground based vehicles, band rejection filtering in the LNA is required. Aviation-quality antennas typically provide an input filter to prevent swamping of the LNA's first RF stage.

Antennas for DGPS

Signals received on the L1 (1575 MHz) frequency from the GPS constellation satellites allow an accuracy within 100 meters laterally. Typically, 15 to 20 meters is being experienced much of the time. These accuracies, though sufficient for most applications, can be significantly improved by Differential GPS.

DGPS can be provided by a variety of methods, and several differential GPS systems are currently being demonstrated at a few airports. Typically, a GPS base station located permanently at an airport receives the same L1 frequency as an approaching aircraft. But the base station compares the position indicated by the satellites (via the L1 frequency) with its own surveyed geographical location to develop GPS correction signals. By transmitting these corrections over the VHF nav or comm bands to the approaching aircraft, accuracies of within less than 1 meter are very practical. Of course, the GPS receiver in the aircraft must be able to incorporate this correction data and the nav and/or comm radios must be able to strip out the data on a standard channel. Antennas are under development that allow reception of both the GPS L1 frequency and the applicable VHF correction data over the data link. These antennas are referred to as VHF/GPS "combination" antennas.

Making the Right Choice

The GPS industry has grown at a terrific pace since about half the satellites were placed in orbit in mid-1991. Receiver manufacturers make GPS receivers, and sometimes make the antennas as well. While these manufacturers usually provide antennas as standard equipment, there will be times when you may want to purchase an external antenna to enhance the performance of a handheld unit. When you decide to use an antenna other than that supplied by the GPS receiver manufacturer, you will want assurance that it will work with your unit.

When in doubt, the manufacturer of the receiver or antenna should be contacted to obtain confirmation of testing that was conducted to validate the effectiveness of the antenna with your particular GPS receiver. Antenna manufacturers usually have test range facilities that support the design of GPS antennas. Because of this capability, the antennas provided by antenna manufacturers are, in some cases, more efficient, the LNAs might draw less current (extending battery life), and the price could be lower.

Loran Antennas

Loran operates on a different frequency than GPS, and thus the antenna placement considerations are quite different. The following information was prepared by Walt Dean, formerly an engineer at ARNAV Systems, and is reprinted here through the courtesy of ARNAV.

First, for those technically inclined, a few words about how loran-receiving antennas work. The elementary receiver antenna is a dipole, with the received signal voltage generated at the terminals at the

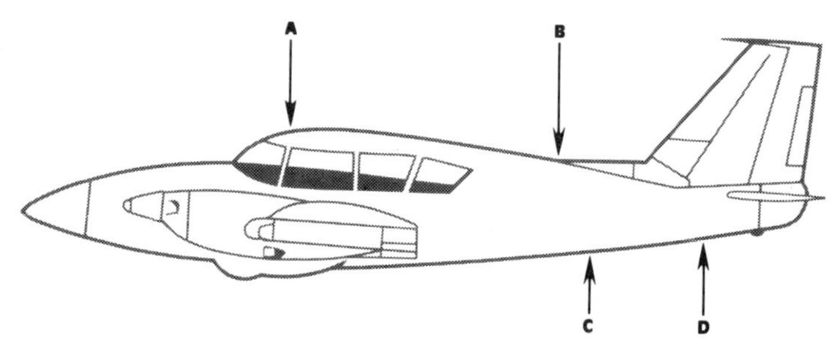

Fig. C-1. Antenna locations for a metal aircraft.

center. The most familiar example of the dipole is the simple TV receiving antenna. At the VHF TV frequency, the antenna is resonant at one-quarter wavelength in each element, so that the electrical impedance seen at the terminals is just right to match the feeder cable.

The wavelength of Loran-C is 3,000 meters, so that all practical receiving antennas are electrically short. This means that the antennas all have a high reactive impedance, which makes them more difficult to couple than resonant antennas. This is why almost all loran receivers use a preamplifier that is located close to the antenna to couple the antenna to the cable to the receiver. The antenna, which is electrically equivalent to a small capacitance, is usually made part of a tuned circuit to limit the bandwidth of the input and match the antenna impedance to the input of the preamp.

Installations in metal aircraft. Because the receiver is usually grounded to the aircraft skin, a whip antenna (which is the type most commonly used) behaves primarily like a grounded monopole. However, because the entire aircraft is so small with respect to a wavelength of the loran signal, the size and shape of the aircraft and location of the antenna can affect its performance. On the bottom-mounted antenna, the ground is at a higher potential than the antenna, which produces a phase inversion in the signals. Fig. C-1 shows the recommended positioning of a loran antenna on a typical fixed-wing aircraft. Top mounting is preferred, as it works better than a bottom mount when the aircraft is on the ground. The top-mounted antenna should be mounted some distance behind the windshield, as this is a common source of precipitation static, which will be discussed later.

If a bottom mount is used, it should be as far to the rear as practical so that the ground clearance is at least three feet. The lack of clearance usually makes it necessary to use a shorter antenna, with the corresponding loss of sensitivity. If the antenna is located too close to

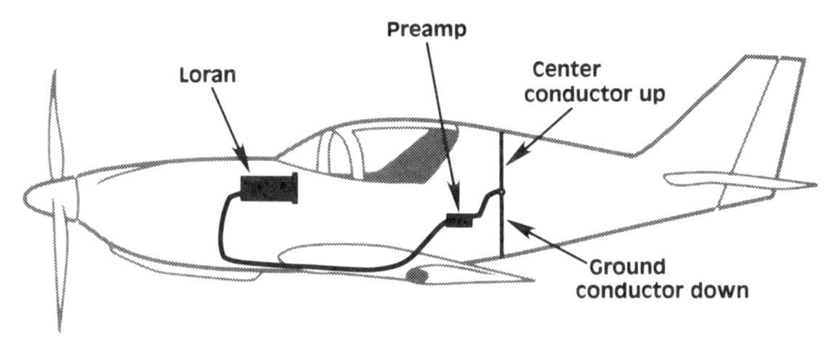

Fig. C-2. Glasair dipole installation

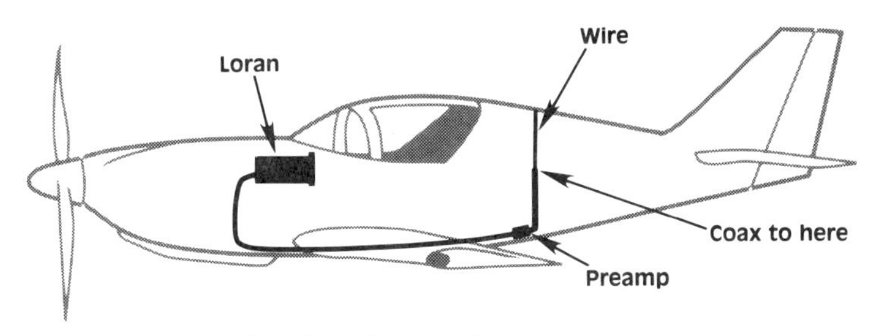

Fig. C-3. Alternate Glasair installation

the ground, the signals will be weaker, and phase distortions may occur, causing errors while on the ground.

Installations in plastic aircraft. The plastic aircraft has no ground plane, such as that found on the metal aircraft, but this is not the disadvantage that many may think it is. Without all that interfering metal, it is easy to make a true dipole and install it in a vertical configuration. Fig. C-2 shows a dipole installation for a loran receiver in a Glasair. The location selected was chosen for its obvious convenience of installation and the fact that it is well removed from outside electrical interferences. Location at least a foot away from the seat is all that is required to avoid any influence from metal there.

Fig. C-3 shows a variation of the dipole that appears to be a monopole but is actually electrically equivalent to the dipole of Fig. C-2. The lower half of the antenna is merely a coax cable, and the shield of the cable acts as the lower half of the dipole, while the extended center conductor is the upper half. This configuration is easy to make: simply measure the available length of the antenna, cut the coax to fit and then strip the shield off the upper half of the coax. If the length of

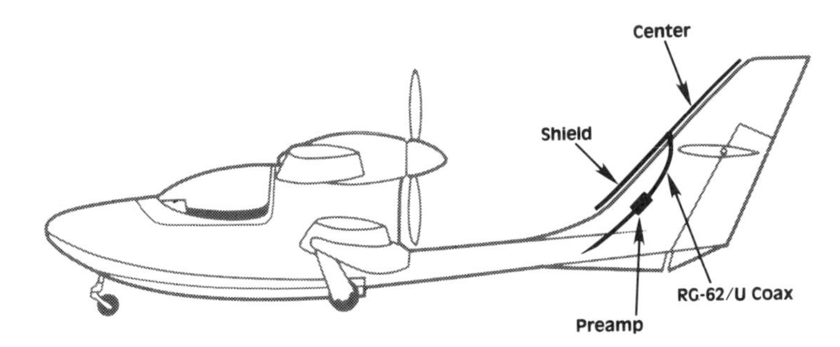

Fig. C-4 Seahawk dipole installation

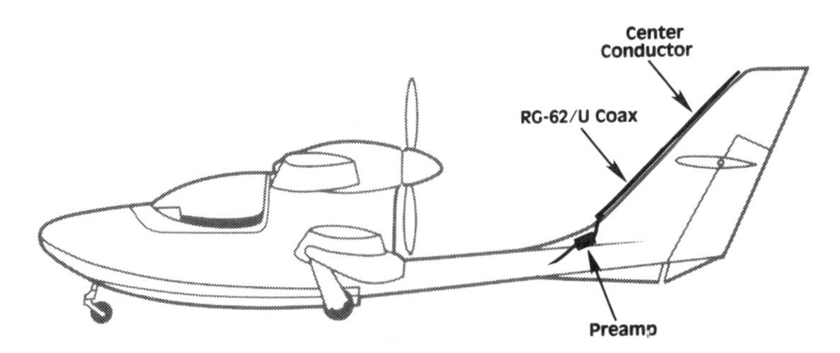

Fig. C-5. Seahawk monopole installation

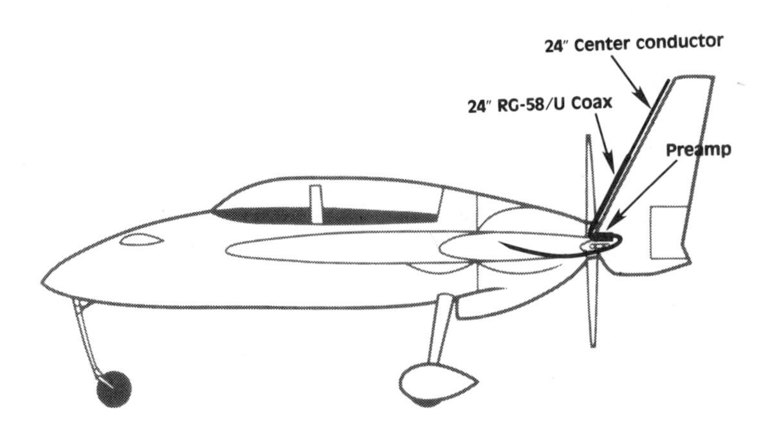

Fig. C-6. Long-EZ installation

the shielded (unstripped) part of the antenna is two feet or less, use RG-58/U cable; if the antenna is longer than that, it is recommended that the RG-62/U cable, which has less shunt capacitance, be used with any of the ARNAV loran installations. The Glasair, because of its engine location, is an easy problem for the antenna installer to solve. Less conventional configurations present more difficult problems. Fig. C-4 illustrates how a dipole was installed in Gary LeGare's Seahawk.

The location in the tail of the Seahawk was chosen because the pusher engine configuration and all the wiring in the cabin make the fuselage an electrically noisy environment. This makes location of an

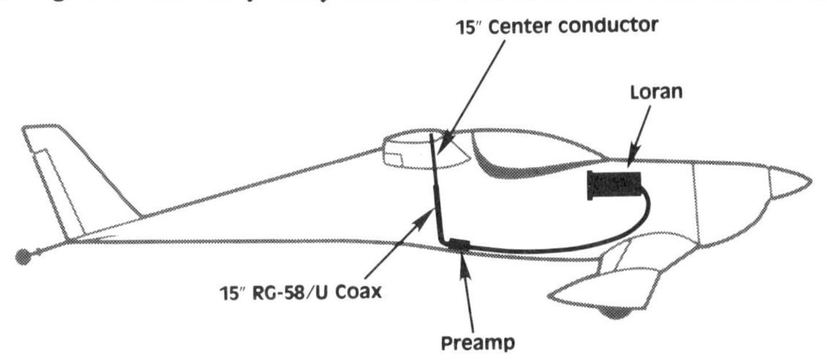

Fig. C-7. Quickie installation.

antenna in the cabin area undesirable. The dipole has been glassed over and is part of the vertical stabilizer. Fig. C-5 shows the monopole variation that makes an excellent alternative to the dipole. Here the length is long enough that RG-62/U coax should be used for the lower portion of the antenna.

About the only possible location for a loran antenna in a Long-EZ is shown in Fig. C-6. Since the antenna coupler is located at the base of the antenna, the long run back to the fuselage is no problem. The only problem may come if strobe lights are used on the wingtips close to the antenna. Cheap strobes have been known to be deadly for the loran.

The Quickie, as shown in Fig. C-7, presents a situation similar to the Glasair's, which means easy. The empty space behind the pilot is nearly ideal for an antenna in the plastic aircraft.

General Antenna Considerations. It is normal for the SNRs of the signals to be determined by the atmospheric conditions, which means it should not be determined by the aircraft. Noise can be picked up from the aircraft either by the antenna or by coupling directly into the receiver. Both are potential problems. The cures for locally generated noise are not always obvious. Noise can be minimized by observing several precautions: Keep the antenna away from electrical noise sources, which can include engine ignition, strobe lights and power cables.

Use a single-point ground for the loran. Multiple ground points may produce ground loops, which can pick up noise.

Wire the loran receiver as directly as possible to the battery, maintaining overload protection.

If noise is still picked up from other equipment on the aircraft, an inductor-capacitor filter should be inserted into the power line. A simple filter should be located as close as possible to the receiver, consisting of an RF choke, 100 MHz or larger, in the positive power lead, and a capacitor, 10 uf or larger, across the receiver input terminals. These can be obtained at any electronics parts supply store.

Installation Checkout Procedures. Once the loran installation is made, it should be checked to see if it has any of the above problems. The general procedures for this are:

Turn on the loran with all other electrical switches off. Observe the signal-to-noise ratios of the signals. Use the signal with the poorest SNR for the rest of the test.

Shut off the loran, start the engine, turn on the loran, re-acquire signals and compare SNR values. Try different engine speeds. Any significant drop in SNR indicates engine noise problems.

Gradually turn on one electrical circuit at a time, watching the loran SNR to see which, if any, of the on-board systems produces noise in the loran.

If troubles are found, additional filtering or additional grounding may be necessary to reduce the interference. This is largely a trial-and-error process, but it is necessary to obtain optimum performance of the loran.

Precipitation Static. This is a problem that requires special consideration. The phenomenon is usually caused by the impact of snow or ice particles on the aircraft that build up an electrical charge. When the charge voltage becomes high enough, corona discharges occur. On metal aircraft, these discharges occur at sharp points on the airframe and produce electrical noise that is particularly strong in the low-frequency range. There can also be discharges between fixed and movable surfaces if there is not a good electrical bonding between them.

Corona can be reduced by use of static wicks that have a number of very fine points and discharge into the air at a much lower voltage than an edge of the aircraft. This lower-voltage discharge produces less noise. An improved version built by Dayton-Granger is the null field discharger, which has two sharp points—one up and the other down. Since they produce equal and opposite fields in the vertical plane, they should not couple any noise into a vertical antenna.

Another source of corona, and thus noise, is any insulating surface on the aircraft. Particularly vulnerable is the windshield, as it receives a higher amount of impacting particles. Charges building up on the windshield arc off to surround metal and produce noise. Plastic decals and metal decals insulated by their adhesive have also been found to produce noise. It is therefore recommended that the antenna be located some distance from the windshield, and that decals be avoided or removed.

Another source of P-static, the charged cloud, is harder to guard against with hardware. These clouds are associated with electrical storms and can produce large amounts of local noise. An obvious solution is to avoid the storms whenever possible.

Summary

The problem of making a suitable loran receiving antenna for a homebuilt aircraft is not difficult to solve. The requirements for metal aircraft are well documented. For plastic aircraft, a simple dipole provides adequate reception, but the location depends on the particular aircraft's configuration. Some simple precautions in installation are required to minimize electrical interference from other aircraft systems and from precipitation static.

Author's Addenda

To add just a bit to Walt Dean's excellent advice, a number of pilots have successfully used a long wire antenna, such as the old-style ADF antenna, strung along the top or bottom of the fuselage, for pulling in loran signals. (However, you cannot use both a loran and an ADF receiver with the same antenna at the same time.)

A word about my own experience with antenna placement. When my first loran, a II Morrow Model 612, was installed on my Tiger, the avionics technician put the straight whip antenna right alongside the comm antenna; they were 4½" apart. I was horrified, because I had always heard that loran and comm antennas should be well separated. However, it worked fine, and there was no loran signal degradation when I transmitted with the comm set.

I kept that antenna placement when I switched to a Northstar M1. Then when I got my KLN 88, Bendix/King recommended a bottom-mounted bent whip antenna, placed as far aft as possible. The manufacturer considered this to be the best location for minimizing precipitation static. But I had a problem at first, consisting of periodic and aggravating losses of signal, even in good reception areas.

After much testing and swapping of parts, it was discovered that the installing technician had made an elementary mistake by failing to adequately prepare the aircraft's surface where the antenna was mounted; he simply didn't remove enough paint to create a good bond. When this was corrected by a Bendix/King technical rep, I was in business. Moral: When you're having an avionics problem, don't automatically blame the equipment.—KC

Appendix D

Directory of Manufacturers

Aircraft Spruce
P.O. Box 424
Fullerton, CA 92632
800-824-1930
FAX: 714-871-7289

ARNAV Systems
P.O. Box 73730
Puyallup, WA 98373
206-848-6060
FAX: 206-848-3555

Artex Aircraft Supplies
P.O. Box 1270
Canby, OR 97103
800-547-8901
FAX: 503-266-3362

Ashtech
1170 Kifer Rd
Sunnyvale, CA 94086
408-524-1400
FAX: 408-524-1500

Bendix/King
400 North Rodgers Road
Olathe, KS 66062
913-782-0400
FAX: 913-791-1302

Ken Brock Mfg.
11852 Western Ave.
Stanton, CA 90680
714-898-4366

BVR
5459 Eleventh Street
Rockford, IL 61125
815-874-2471
FAX: 815-874-4415

Century Flight Systems
P.O. Box 610
Mineral Wells, TX 76067
817-325-2517

Comant Industries
12920 Park Street
Santa Fe Springs, CA 90670
310-946-6694
FAX: 310-946-5150

Communications Specialists
426 West Taft Avenue
Orange, CA 92665-4296
800-854-0547
FAX: 714-974-3420

Eventide
One Alsan Way
Little Ferry, NJ 07643
800-446-7878; 201-641-1200
FAX: 201-641-1640

Flight Products International
P.O.B. 1558
Kalispell, MT 59901
800-526-1231

Garmin
9875 Widmer Road
Lenexa, KS 66215
800-800-1020; 913-599-1515
FAX: 913-599-2103

Icarus Instruments
7585 Washington Blvd., Ste
108
Baltimore, MD 21227
301-799-9497
FAX: 301-799-8320

ICOM America
2380 116th Avenue N.E.
Belleview, WA 98004
206-454-8155
FAX: 206-450-6079

Lone Star Aviation
1306 Tatum Dr.
Arlington, TX 76012
817-548-7768
FAX: 817-261-8692

Lowrance Avionics
12000 East Skelly Drive
Tulsa, OK 74128
918-437-6881

Magellan Systems
960 Overland Court
San Dimas, CA 91773
909-394-5000
FAX: 909-394-7050

McCoy Avionics
6145 Scherers Place
Dublin, OH 43017
800-654-8124; 614-888-8080
FAX: 614-889-8283

MentorPlus
P.O.B. 356
Aurora, OR 97002
503-678-1431
FAX: 503-678-1480

Memtec
19B Keewaydin Dr
Salem, NH 03079
603-893-8080
FAX: 603-893-8699

Mid-Continent Instrument
7706 East Osie
Wichita, KS 67207
800-821-1212; 316-683-5532
FAX: 316-683-1861

Narco Avionics
270 Commerce Drive
Fort Washington, PA 19034
800-223-3636; 215-643-2905
FAX: 215-643-0197

Northstar Avionics
30 Sudbury Road
Acton, MA 01720
800-628-4487; 508-897-6600
FAX: 508-897-8264

Peacock Systems
Hanscom Field
Bedford, MA 01730
617-274-8218
FAX: 617-274-8130

Ross Engineering
12505-E Starkey Road
Largo, FL 34643
813-536-1226
FAX: 813-535-4248

Shadin
14280 North 23rd Ave.
Plymouth, MN 55447
800-328-0584
FAX: 612-557-9195

Sigma-Tek
1001 Industrial Road
Augusta, KS 67010
316-775-6373
FAX: 316-775-1416

Sony
1 Sony Drive
Park Ridge, NJ 07656-8003
201-930-1000
FAX: 201-930-7179

Sporty's Pilot Shop
Clermont Airport
Batavia, OH 45103
800-543-8633
FAX: 513-732-6560

S-TEC
Route 4, Bldg. 946
Mineral Wells, TX 76067-9990
800-872-7832; 817-325-9406
FAX: 817-325-3904

Terra
3520 Pan American Fwy, N.E.
Albuquerque, NM 87107
505-884-2321
FAX: 505-884-2384

TKM
14811 North 73rd Street
Scottsdale, AZ 85260
602-991-5351
FAX: 602-991-3759

Trimble
2105 Donley Drive
Austin, TX 78758
800-487-4662
FAX: 512-836-9413

II Morrow
P.O. Box 13549
Salem, OR 97309
503-581-8101
FAX: 503-364-2138

VAL Avionics
P.O. Box 13025
Salem, OR 97309
800-255-1511; 503-370-9429
FAX: 503-370-9885

Wag-Aero
1216 North Road
Lyons, WI 53148
414-763-9586
FAX: 414-763-7595

Zycom
18 Loblolly Lane
Wayland, MA 01778
800-955-6466; 508-358-5052
FAX: 508-358-4988

Appendix E

Glossary of Acronyms, Abbreviations & Terms

ADF Automatic Direction Finder.

Angular deviation In VOR navigation, the further the aircraft from the VOR station, the greater the distance between degrees.

ARINC Aeronautical Radio, Inc., an organization that sets certain size and technological standards for avionics.

ARTCC Air Route Traffic Control Center.

ATC Air Traffic Control.

ASF Additional Secondary (Phase) Factor; the amount of delay in a loran signal's speed as it travels over land. The amount of delay is measurable and is accounted for in the more sophisticated loran sets.

ATIS Automatic Terminal Information Service; a recording of terminal area information of a non-control nature, available on specified radio frequencies.

AWOS Automatic Weather Observing/Reporting System.

Azimuth dial A display of horizontal angular direction.

Baseline An imaginary straight line between a loran master station and a secondary.

Baseline extension Continuation of a baseline beyond a station, an area of degraded loran accuracy.

Blink A special code emitted by a loran transmitter to indicate an abnormality in its transmission.

BNC Bayonet Naval Connector; used to connect radio and antenna cables.

C/A code Coarse/Acquisition code; a sequence of modulations that provide a GPS signal of somewhat degraded accuracy for use by civilians.

CDI Course Deviation Indicator.

CDU Control/Display Unit.

Chain A group of loran stations consisting of a master and two to five secondary or slave stations.

Channel On a GPS receiver, the circuitry necessary to tune the signal from a single GPS satellite.

Class B airspace Formerly known as a TCA, or Terminal Control Area; positive controlled airspace established at busy airports. An ATC clearance is required before entry.

Class C airspace Formerly known as an ARSA, or Airport Radar Service Area; an area of airspace around an airport. Two-way communication with the controller is required before entry.

Comm Communications.

Cone of confusion The cone-shaped area over a VOR station in which the signal is ambiguous.

Control segment A worldwide network of GPS monitoring and control stations that enhance the accuracy of satellite positions and their clocks.

CRT Cathode ray tube, used in displays of weather avoidance systems and some upper-end GPS receivers.

CTAF Common Traffic Advisory Frequency. At controlled airports, this is the control tower frequency; at uncontrolled airports, it would usually be a unicom frequency.

Cycle slip or **cycle error** In loran, selection by the loran's computer of an incorrect cycle, which it is using for time-distance computations. In GPS, a discontinuity in the measurement of the GPS signal resulting from a temporary loss of signal lock-on by the receiver.

Database In loran and GPS receivers, a listing of waypoints. A factory database consists of software that contains programmed data such as lat/lon coordinates of airports, navaids, and other waypoints in permanent memory.

DG Directional Gyro.

Differential GPS A technique to provide system accuracy by determining positioning error at a known location and subsequently transmitting a correction to users of the system operating in the same area.

DME Distance Measuring Equipment; computerized onboard radio equipment that interrogates a VORTAC to provide distance and groundspeed.

Dot matrix In an avionics display, a series of dots that form alphanumeric messages.

ECD Envelope-to-Cycle Discrepancy; an indication that the loran receiver has focused on the wrong part of the broadcast pulse envelope.

ECDI Electronic Course Deviation Indicator. ECDIs are included in the displays of loran and GPS receivers and some VHF handhelds.

ELT Emergency Locator Transmitter; a radio transmitter required on all aircraft, designed to broadcast a signal on emergency frequencies if the plane crashes.

Emission delay The time lapse between the start of the loran master station pulse and the start of the secondary station pulse groups. Each secondary has a different emission delay period.

Envelope The shape of a loran radio pulse.

Ephemeris Data transmitted by a satellite updating its position.

ETA Estimated Time of Arrival.

ETE Estimated Time Enroute.

Extended range A function that alters a loran set's method of signal tracking to enhance reception in fringe areas.

FAA Federal Aviation Administration.

FBO Fixed Base Operator.

FSS Flight Service Station.

Gas plasma A type of display used on some comm radios and electronic CDIs.

Glideslope An angular descent path, provided on an aircraft's final approach by an ILS or a visual light system.

Great circle A circle about the earth's surface whose plane extends through the earth's center. A great circle route is the shortest distance between two points on earth.

GRI Group Repetition Interval; the fixed time lapse, in microseconds, between the beginning of one master pulse group to the next. This interval, with one zero dropped, becomes the designator of the chain; e.g., a GRI of 89,700 microseconds is designated GRI 8970. GRI is sometimes used as a synonym for chain.

Groundwave A radio wave traveling along the surface of the earth; used for loran navigation.

HSI Horizontal Situation Indicator; an instrument that combines the functions of a DG and a VOR/LOC/GS course deviation indicator.

Hyperbolic A type of curve shaped in such a way that the difference between the distances from any point on it to two fixed points is the same for all points on the curve.

IFR Instrument Flight Rules.

ILS Instrument Landing System; a precision instrument approach system using localizer and glideslope signals.

Ionosphere A band of charged particles in orbit 80 to 120 miles above the earth's surface.

KHz Kilohertz; a frequency of 1000 cycles per second.

Lat/lon Latitude and longitude.

Latitude The distance north or south of the equator, measured in degrees, minutes and seconds.

L-band The group of radio frequencies extending from 390 MHz to 1550 MHz. The GPS carrier frequencies (1227.6 MHz and 1575.42 MHz) are in the L band.

LCD Liquid Crystal Display, used on some GPS, loran, and comm radios, particularly where cost and power usage is an important consideration.

LED Light-Emitting Diode, a type of display used instead of LCD (above); LED is more readable than LCD, but the cost and power usage is higher.

Leg A route of flight between two waypoints.

Linear deviation A constant course deviation, normally expressed in nautical miles; used for parallel offset navigation by loran or RNAV.

Load present position The process of defining as a waypoint an aircraft's current position.

LOP Line Of Position; a hyperbolic line between two loran stations, the curve of which is determined by their TDs.

Longitude The distance east or west of the prime meridian at Greenwich, expressed in degrees, minutes, and seconds.

Loran Long Range Navigation system, utilizing low frequency radio signals.

Lubber line A reference mark on a compass or other navigational instrument.

Ma Milliamp; one thousandth of an ampere.

Mag/var Magnetic variation.

MEA Minimum enroute altitude; the lowest published altitude between radio fixes that assures signal coverage and obstacle clearance.

Meridian Line of longitude.

MHz Megahertz; one million cycles per second.

Microseconds Millionths of a second.

Multi-sensor systems Navigation systems that utilize more than one type of radionavigation input (loran, GPS, etc.) to determine position.

Nav Navigation.

Navaid Navigational aid, such as a VOR station.

NDB Non-Directional Beacon, a type of radio navigation station.

NiCad Nickel cadmium; used in rechargeable batteries.

NM Nautical Miles.

NOS National Ocean Survey; a division of National Oceanic and Atmospheric Administration, which publishes aviation charts.

OBS Omnibearing Selector; knob on the CDI used to select the desired bearing to or from a VOR station.

Oscillator In loran, a precise clock used by transmitters and receivers to coordinate TDs.

Page The information shown on a display at one time.

Parallel Line of latitude.

Parallel offset A function that sets a course parallel to a reference course.

P-code A sequence of modulations utilized for the Precise Positioning GPS system; restricted mostly to military use.

PEP Peak Envelope Power; a measurement of transmitter output.

Phase coding A pattern of loran pulses that enables the receiver to distinguish between the master and secondary stations.

Preamp Pre-amplifier, sometimes called a coupler. Boosts signals at a loran receiver's antenna.

Precession Movement of the spin axis of a gyro away from its original alignment, resulting in indication error.

Precise Positioning Service (PPS) GPS transmissions based on the P-code, primarily for military use.

Propagation error Degradation of loran accuracy caused by the slowing of the loran signal as it travels over the ground. The amount of the error depends on the terrain; there is virtually no slowing over water. Most airborne loran sets compensate for propagation error.

Pseudo-random code In GPS, a signal similar to random noise, but actually a very complicated repeated pattern of ones and zeroes.

Radial A magnetic bearing from a VOR station.

RAIM Receiver Autonomous Integrity Monitoring; a cross-checking method by which a GPS receiver can determine that its position information is accurate. This can be done via either an additional satellite or another navigation system, such as loran. RAIM is required for IFR certification of GPS receivers.

RF Radio Frequency.

RMI Radio Magnetic Indicator; a navigation instrument that displays magnetic heading as well as ADF and VOR bearings.

RNAV Area Navigation; although there are several types of area navigation systems used in aviation, the acronym RNAV usually refers to the system that utilizes a computer, VOR receiver and DME to establish waypoints based on radial and distance from VORTACs.

RNAV Direct An IFR clearance direct to a waypoint, usually bypassing Victor airways; requires IFR-certified equipment such as RNAV, GPS, or loran.

Scalloping Side-to-side needle movement on a VOR CDI, due to reflected or secondary signals.

Secondary Loran slave station.

Selective Availability Degradation of GPS signals for security purposes by the Department of Defense.

Signal tracking error Inaccurate loran information caused by the receiver tracking the wrong station(s).

Skywave A radio signal reflected back to earth by the ionosphere. Although loran receivers are designed to reject skywaves for normal operations, one manufacturer uses skywaves for extended range.

Slant range distance The distance computed by DME between an aircraft and a VORTAC, based on the time intervals of radio pulses. The distance includes the height of the plane above the station.

Slant range error The discrepancy in a DME distance readout due to the aircraft's height above the station.

SNR Signal-to-Noise Ratio; the relationship of a radio signal to unwanted interference.

Specific range An aircraft's range with reference to specific factors, such as power setting, groundspeed, etc.

Standard Positioning Service (SPS) GPS transmissions utilizing the C/A code for civilian use.

Station geometry Geographical relationships of loran stations to each other.

TACAN Tactical Air Navigation; A UHF military navaid that provides aircraft with bearing and distance to the TACAN station.

TD Time Difference; the difference in time of arrival (in microseconds) of the loran signals from a master and a slave station.

TPA Traffic Pattern Altitude.

Transceiver A combined radio transmitter and receiver.

Triad A master station and two secondaries, used for loran navigational computations.

Triangulation A trigonometric rule stating that if two sides of a triangle and the angle they form are known, the third side of the triangle can be determined.

TSO Technical Standard Order; a set of FAA specifications for technical and environmental performance of avionics.

TWEB Transcribed Weather Broadcast.

UF Microfarad; one millionth of a farad, a unit of electrical capacitance.

Unicom VHF Communications using an advisory frequency for information on landing conditions at an uncontrolled airport, requests for fuel service, etc.

UTC Universal Coordinated Time (Zulu), also referred to as Greenwich Mean Time.

Vacuum fluorescent A type of display used on a few GPS receivers. It offers the advantage of a power drain that is considerably lower than LED, but its drawback is a greater loss of clarity in direct sunlight.

VFR Visual Flight Rules.

VNAV Vertical Navigation guidance; computed by some GPS and loran receivers to provide a constant ascent or descent path.

VOR Very high frequency Omnidirectional Range.

VOR/LOC VOR/Localizer receiver or CDI.

VOR/LOC/GS VOR/Localizer/Glideslope receiver or CDI.

VORTAC Combined VOR and TACAN facility.

Waypoint A navigational point of reference, or fix, primarily defined by latitude and longitude.

Index

A

A300 (Sporty's Pilot Shop handheld), 144
AC-U-KWIK, 155
Additional Secondary phase Factor (ASF), 23
ADF, interfacing with Argus moving map display, 111–112
AEA (Aircraft Electronics Association), 148
AEROplan GPS V, 116–117
Air Chart System, 45–46
Aircraft Electronics Association (AEA), 148
Aircraft Spruce, 169
air data systems and fuel computers, 56, 63, 120–121
Airports of Baja California and Northwest Mexico, 157
airspace alerts (SUA), 50
air temperature from fuel flow/air data systems, 63
altimeters, conventional, errors in, 31, 36
altitude encoders, 31, 63
angular deviation, 18
antennas
  for DGPS units, 160–161
  for GPS units, 28, 158–161
  for handheld GPS units, 92
  for handheld radios, 139
  for loran, 161–168
AOPA'S Aviation USA, 156
Apollo 920 handheld GPS, 91, 93–96
Apollo altitude encoder, 63
approaches. *See also* IFR approaches
  GPS, 33, 35–36, 41–44
  loran, 33, 35
  overlay type, 36
  precision, 36–37
ARC radio replacements, 132
Argus 3000/5000/7000 (Eventide moving map displays), 52, 109–114
ARNAV, 169
  fuel computer, 120–121
  GPS and multi-sensor units, 80–81
  lorans, 33
Artex Aircraft Supplies, 169
  ELT-to-GPS/loran interface, 122
ASF (Additional Secondary phase Factor), 23, 53
Ashtech, 88, 169
  Altair AV-12 GPS, 47, 88–89
atomic clocks, on GPS satellites, 30
autopilot, CDI/HSI interface to GPS/loran, 122
AV-12 (Ashtech), 47
Aviator's Data Log, 155
avionics
  by mail order, 149–150
  caring for, 150–151
  choosing, 15–16
  cooling, 150
  installing, 145–151
  master switch for, 151
  trade-in allowances for, 146
avionics shops, choosing, 145–151

B

Baja Bush Pilots, 157
baseline extension, 24, 25
batteries
  for handheld GPS units, 92
  for handheld radios, 140–141
Bendix/King, 74, 169
  GPS/comm, 137–138
  handheld radio, 142–143
  loran and GPS, 33, 74–79
  nav/comms, 125, 126, 127–129
blink, 26
bootstrap, 63
Brock, Ken, Mfg., 143, 169
Burrell, Gary, 70

BVR, 169
BVR CDI series, 123

C

C1 (Northstar remote comm), 82, 130
Canadian Marconi, 81
Carlson, Doug, 42, 72
CDI (course deviation indicator)
  ECDI (electronic), 126, 131
  electronic in GPS or loran, 49
  interfacing to GPS/loran, 122
  on II Morrow Flybuddy GPS, 57
Century Flight Systems, 169
certification. *See* IFR certification
Cessna/ARC radio replacements, 132
chains (of loran stations), 21–25, 53
channels on GPS units, 53
Cinema Air, 38
Class A1/A2/B1/B2 specifications (TSO C129), 36
climb/descent angle computation with VNAV, 50–51
clocks
  for ETA, 19, 49
  on GPS satellites, 30
Collins Micro Line (now S-TEC radios), 134–135
COM 760 TSO (VAL radio), 131–132
COM 810+/811+ (Narco comm units), 130
Comant Industries, 158, 169
comms. *See also* nav/comms
  sufficiency with GPS or loran for nav, 15
Communications Specialists, 143, 169
computers
  with moving map software, 108, 115–119
  using with II Morrow handheld GPS, 92
cone of confusion, 18
cooling your avionics, 150
coordinates. *See* Latitude/Longitude
Co-Pilot and Co-Pilot Remote (Memtec moving map), 117–118
crossed-slot GPS antennas, 159
Crown radios (Bendix/King), 12
CRT (cathode ray tube), 46, 52
CW (Carrier Wave), 141

D

databases
  in GPSs and lorans, 47–48
  on moving maps, 108
  PC-updatable for handheld GPS units, 94
  user-replaceable for GPS/loran, 48, 56, 62, 66, 71, 75–76, 80, 83, 85, 88
  user-replaceable for moving maps, 110
data ports, 54
Dean, Walt, 161
density altitude from fuel flow/air data systems, 63
Department of Defense (DoD), 31
descent guidance with VNAV, 51
Desert Storm and Selective Availability, 32
DGPS (Differential GPS), 32
  antennas for, 160–161
Digiflo-L (Shadin fuel computer), 120
displays
  on GPS or loran units, 46–47
  on nav/comms, 125–126
DME, 19–20
DoD (Department of Defense), 31
Dzus rail-mount systems, 46, 64, 70, 73, 81

E

ECD (envelope-to-cycle discrepancy), 26
ECDI (electronic course deviation indicators), 126, 131
ELS-10 (Artex ELT), 122
ELT interface with GPS, 122
emergencies
  and ELTs, 122
  and handhelds, 91, 139
  and nearest airport/waypoint feature, 50
encoding altimeters, 31
envelope-to-cycle discrepancy (ECD), 26
ephemeris data, 30
Escort II (Narco radio), 124, 129
ETA
  from DME, 19
  from GPS or loran, 23, 49
ETE
  from DME, 19
  from GPS or loran, 21, 23, 40, 49

Eventide, 169
moving map displays, 109–114

F

FAA, 37
F/ADC (Shadin fuel/air data computer), 68, 121
fans for avionics cooling, 150
FC-10 (Arnav fuel computer), 120–121
filtering of RF, 158, 160
Flight Guide, 156
Flightmate Pro (Trimble GPS), 100–104
Flightmate Pro SE (Trimble GPS), 104
flight plans, 49
Flight Products International, 108, 169
flip-flop feature, 125
FliteMap (MentorPlus moving map software), 118
Flybrary database, 56
Flybuddy GPS (II Morrow), 56–60
Flybuddy (II Morrow loran), 33, 56
FMS 5000 (ARNAV multi-sensor unit), 80–81
FMS 7000 (ARNAV multi-sensor Dzus-rail mount unit), 81
frequencies
used by GPS satellites, 28, 31
used by loran stations, 21
used by VOR transmitters, 17
frequency management
advantages with GPS or loran, 50
with GPS/comms, 15, 137
on handhelds, 140
on nav/comms, 125–126, 140
FSDOs, 37
fuel computers and air data systems, 56, 63, 120–121

G

GARMIN, 70, 170
GPSs, 37
handheld GPS, 91, 104
95 XL handheld GPS unit, 97–100
portable moving map, 52
shooting GPS approaches, 42
Genese moving map, 119
Glasair loran antenna placement, 163, 165
Global Positioning System. *See* GPS (Global Positioning System)
GPS 55 AVD (Garmin GPS), 100, 104
GPS-60 (Northstar GPS), 82, 84
GPS 95 AVD (Garmin GPS), 97, 98
GPS 100 AVD (Garmin GPS), 100
GPS 150 (Garmin GPS), 70
GPS 155 (Garmin GPS), 70, 71–73
GPS 165 (Garmin GPS/Dzus-rail mount), 70
GPS-600 (Northstar GPS), 82, 84
GPS 900 (Narco GPS), 88
GPS 5000 (Peacock GPS), 116
GPS/comms
advantages, 15, 137
models, 125, 137–138
GPS (Global Positioning System). *See also* moving map displays
accessories, 120–123
approaches, 33, 35–36
cost considerations, 45–46
database considerations, 47–48
dimensions and diplay considerations, 46–47
handheld models *(begin on page 92)*
IFR certifiability, 33
importance of verifying, 21, 25, 26, 152
learning curve considerations, 54
navigation feature considerations, 49–53
panel-mounted models *(begin on page 55)*
signal acquisition considerations, 53–54
system description, 28–32
versus loran, 33–34
GPS-Loran Navigation Atlas, 156–157
GRI. *See also* chains
described, 22–23
groundspeed
from DME, 19
from loran or GPS, 21, 23, 39, 49

H

handheld GPS units
advantages, 91–92
antennas for, 158–161
GARMIN 95 XL, 97–100
Lowrance Avionics, 107

handheld GPS units (*continued*)
Magellan, 104–105
Sony, 106–107
Trimble, 100–104, 107
II Morrow, 92–96
handheld nav/comms
features and considerations, 139–141
models, 141–144
Henry, Jerry, 38
high-altitude (H) VOR, 17
HSI interface with GPS/loran/moving map systems, 111, 113

I

IC-A2/A20/A21 (ICOM handhelds), 141–142
IC-A200 (ICOM radio), 132
Icarus Instruments, 170
serializer (transponder-to-GPS interface), 121
ICOM America, 132, 141–142, 170
ICS Plus (radio), 135–136
IFR approaches. *See also* approaches
DME and RNAV for, 19, 20
with GPS, 33, 35–36
GPS and RAIM (receiver autonomous integrity monitoring), 34
NDB for, 20
need for VOR receivers for, 15
IFR certification
advantages over VFR sets, 40
GPS advancing on loran, 33
versus certifiability, 37–39
IFR operations. *See also* approaches; IFR approaches
clearances via handheld radio, 139
with GPS or loran, 35, 39–40
II Morrow. *See under* II Morrow (*spelled as in "two"*)
IND-350A/351A (TEC LINE indicators), 135
INMARSATs, 32
Insight Strike Finder interface for Argus moving map displays, 112
installation
of antennas, 158–168
of avionics, 145–151
instrument approaches. *See* approaches; IFR approaches
intersections
in loran or GPS databases, 47
navigating to, with GPS or loran, 39–40
IPS-360 (Sony handheld GPS), 106
IPS-760 (Sony handheld GPS), 91, 106–107

J

JeppGuide, 156
Jet routes in databases, 47, 83

K

Kao, Min, 70
King Radio. *See also* Bendix/King
replacements for, 132–134
KLN 88 (Bendix/King loran), 33, 74
KLN 90A and B (Bendix/King GPS), 45, 47, 74–79
KLX 135 GPS/Comm, 125, 129, 137–138
KN 53 (Bendix/King radio), 128
KX 99 (Bendix/King handheld radio), 142–143
KX 125 (Bendix/King radio), 128
KX 155/165 (Bendix/King radios), 126, 128
KX 170/175 King radio replacements, 132–134
KY 96A/196A/97A/197A (Bendix/King radios), 125, 129

L

LapMap (Peacock Systems moving map), 115–116
latitude/longitude
guides for looking up, 155–157
system of, 152–154
as used by loran/GPS, 23
LCA 200 (Ross multi-sensor unit), 89–90
LCD (liquid crystal display), 46, 52, 59
LED (light-emitting diode), 46
linear deviation, 18
LNA (low noise amplifier), 158
Lone Star Aviation, 79, 170
Long-EZ loran antenna placement, 164, 165
longitude. *See* latitude/longitude
LOP (line of position)
in GPS system, 28–29
in loran systems, 22, 24, 25
loran. *See also* moving map displays
accessories and equipment interfaces, 120–123
advantages and disadvantages, 21, 33–34

loran (*continued*)
antenna installation considerations, 161–168
approaches, 33, 35
chains, 21–25
cost considerations, 45–46
diagnostic messages, 25–26
dimensions and diplay considerations, 46–47
future of, 33–34
IFR certifiability, 33
importance of verifying, 21, 25, 26, 152
learning curve considerations, 54
navigation feature considerations, 49–53
panel-mounted models (*begin on page 55*)
signal acquisition considerations, 53–54
low-altitude (L) VOR, 17
low noise amplifier (LNA), 158
Lowrance Avionics, 170
handheld GPS unit, 107

M

M1 (Northstar loran), 81
M2 (Northstar loran/multi-sensor unit), 82, 84
M3 (Northstar loran/multi-sensor unit), 82–84
MAC 1700/1700VT (McCoy radios), 133–134
McCoy Avionics, 170
handheld, 125
nav/comms, 133–134
McCoy, Phil, 133
Magellan Systems, 85, 170
GPSs, 85–87
handheld GPS unit, 104–105
magnetic variation, 53–54
mail order avionics, 149–150
manufacturers, directory of, 169–171
Map 7000 (Magellan handheld GPS), 104–105
Mark 12D/12E (Narco radios), 125, 126, 130
master avionics switch, 151
master loran stations, 22
MD 40-60 (Mid-Continent CDI), 123
Memtec, 117–118, 170
MentorPlus, 170
FliteMap, 118
meridians. *See also* Latitude/Longitude
described, 152
MESA/MSA feature, 50
MFD 5000 (ARNAV cockpit management system/moving map display), 114–115
Microflo-L (Shadin fuel computer), 120
Micro Line (S-TEC radios), 134
microstrip patch GPS antennas, 159
Mid-Continent Instruments, 123, 170
Miniflo-L (Shadin fuel computer), 120
Minimum Enroute Safe Altitude (MESA), 50
Minimum Safe Altitude (MSA), 50
Model 3000 (Icarus serializer transponder-to-GPS interface), 121
Morrow, Ray, 55, 80
moving map displays
in handheld GPS units, 91, 95, 98, 104
independent panel-mounted or PC-based, 108–119
in panel-mounted GPS or loran units, 51–53, 78, 88, 108
multi-sensor systems, 55
MX 11 COMM (TKM radio), 133
MX-170B (TKM radio), 125, 132
MX-300/300V/385 (TKM radios), 125, 132–133

N

Narco Avionics, 87, 170
GPS and multi-sensor units, 87–88
nav/comms, 124, 125, 126, 129–130
replacements for older sets, 132–133
National Ocean Survey Airport/Facility Directory, 155–156
Nav 5000 (Magellan GPS), 104, 105
nav/comms
handheld models, 139–144
importance for IFR, 15
panel-mounted models, 127–136
NCS 812 (Narco nav/comm), 130
NDB for IFR approaches, 20
nearest airport/waypoint feature, 50
NMC (Nav Management Computer on II Morrow GPS), 60

NMS (II Morrow multi-sensor unit), 60
Northstar Avionics, 81, 170
  GPS/comm (SmartComm), 84, 125, 130, 138
  lorans, 33

O

1 + 1 and 1 + 1/2 systems, 124
oscillator (loran), 22
overlay approaches, 36, 42
owners' manuals
  advantage of well-designed, 54, 60, 64, 69, 78, 86
  importance of studying, 16, 26, 149

P

pages (on GPS and loran set displays), 47
parallel offset, 51
parallels. *See* latitude/longitude
P-code, 31
Peacock Systems, 115–116, 170
PEP (peak envelope power), 141
Pilot's Guide to California Airports, 157
Pilot's Guide to Southwestern Airports, 157
pilot's operating handbooks. *See* owner's manuals
portable units. *See* handhelds
power considerations
  for handheld GPS units, 92
  for handheld radios, 140–141
  for nav/comms, 124
precipitation static, and antenna installation, 166–167
Precise Positioning Service (PPS), 31
precision approaches, 36–37
PRONAV. *See* GARMIN
pseudo-random code, 29
P-static, 166–167
pulse
  of GPS signal, 29
  of loran signal, 22, 26
  of VORTAC, 19
PYXIS IPS-360 (Sony handheld GPS), 106

Q

quadrifilar GPS antennas, 158–159
Quickie loran antenna placement, 165

R

radio shops, choosing, 145–151
Radio Systems Technology, nav/comm, 136
RAIM (receiver autonomous integrity monitoring), 34
remote ranging, 49–50
repair considerations, 146–147, 148
RF filtering, 158, 160
RMI, readout on radio, 126
RNAV, 19, 20
"RNAV direct" routing, 20, 39
Ross Engineering, 89, 170
  loran and GPS, 89–90
RST-572 (RST nav/comm), 136
RST. *See* Radio Systems Technology

S

scalloping, 18
Seahawk loran antenna placement, 164, 165
searching for nearest airport/waypoint, 50
secondaries (loran stations), 22
Sectional charts, 153
Selective Availability, 32, 33, 37, 105
Senterfitt's New Baja Bush Pilots, 157
serializers (transponder-to-GPS interface), 121
1700/1700VT (McCoy radios), 133–134
Shadin, 170
  fuel flow/air data systems, 63, 68, 120
shops, choosing for installation of avionics, 145–151
Sigma-Tek, 171
signals
  DME, 19
  GPS, 53
  loran, 21, 22, 25, 53
  VOR, 17–19
signal-to-noise ratio (SNR), 25, 165, 166
simulator (training) mode, 54, 64
SkyNav 5000 (Magellan GPS), 85–87
slant range distance/error, 19

SmartComm (Northstar GPS/comm), 84, 125, 130, 138
SNR (signal-to-noise ratio), 25, 165, 166
Sony, 171
handheld GPS unit, 106–107
Special Use Airspace feature (SUA), 50, 52
Sporty's Pilot Shop, 144, 171
Standard Positioning Service (SPS), 31
Star*Nav NS 9000 (Narco multi-sensor unit), 87–88
Star 5000 (ARNAV GPS), 81
S-TEC, 134–135, 171
Stites, John, 158
Stormscope with Argus interface, 111, 112–113
Strike Finder (Insight), interface for Argus moving map displays, 112
SUA (Special Use Airspace) alerts, 50
switches, master avionics, 151

T

TACAN, 17
TDs (time differences)
for GPS signals, 30
for loran signals, 22, 26
TEC LINE nav/comms, 134–135
terminal (T) VOR, 17
Terra, 89, 171
GPS, 89
handheld, 144
nav/comms, 130–131
TGPS 400 D (Terra GPS), 89
3-D positioning with GPS, 31
TKM, 132, 171
TN 200/200D (Terra radios), 130
TNL-1000DC (Trimble GPS), 70
TNL-1000 (Trimble GPS), 70
TNL-2000A and T (Trimble GPS units), 69–70
TNL-2100T (Trimble GPS/Dzus-rail mount), 70
TNL-3000T (Trimble multi-sensor unit), 65–70
II Morrow. *See under* II Morrow (*spelled as in "two"*)
TPX 720 (Terra handheld), 144
TR-720 (Communications Specialists handheld), 143
TRADE-A-PLANE, 149
trade-in allowances, 146
training considerations, 54
training mode, 54, 64
transponder output, interfacing to GPS, 121
Trimble, 64, 171
handheld GPS, 100–104, 107
multi-sensor systems and GPS, 64–70
Trimble, Charles, 64
Tri-Nav (Terra ECDI), 131
Tripboard (Flight Products International mounting system), 108
true airspeed from fuel flow/air data systems, 63
TSOs
C60b, 35
C115a, 35
C129, 36
upgrading to meet standards of, 45
TWEB (transcribed weather broadcast), 19
2-D positioning from GPS, 31
II Morrow, 171
altitude encoder, 63
handheld GPS units, 92–96
panel-mounted lorans and GPS units, 55–64
portable moving maps, 52
2001 GPS (II Morrow), 60–64
TX 720D/760D (Terra radios), 130–131
TX 3200 (Terra comm), 131

U

underlying approaches, 36, 42
updates/upgrades
for GPS/loran or moving maps. *See* databases
to meet standards of TSOs, 45
for nav or comm units. *See individual model numbers*
user-friendliness, 54, 55
user-replaceable databases for GPS/loran, 48, 56, 62, 71, 75–76, 80, 83, 85, 88
user's manuals. *See* owner's manuals
user waypoints, 48

V

VAL Avionics, 171
radio, 131–132
VHF-251/253 (TEC LINE comms), 135
VHF nav/comms. *See* nav/comms
Victor airways in databases, 47, 83
VIR-351 (TEC LINE nav/comms), 134–135

VNAV, 50–51
voice synthesizing radio, 134
VOR, 17–19
VOR-DME, 17
VOR/LOC indicators, 135
VORTAC, 17, 19, 20

W

WAC charts, 153
Wag-Aero, 135–136, 171
warnings
  provided by cockpit management system, 114–115
  provided by external CDIs, 122
  provided by GPSs, 49
  provided by lorans, 25, 26, 49
warranties
  on installation work, 146–147
  on lorans and GPSs, 46
  on mail-ordered units, 150
  on repairs, 148
waypoints
  creatable by user, 48
  in databases, 47–48
winds aloft feature, 51
wind speed/direction from fuel flow/air data systems, 63

Z

Zycom, 116, 171

Laugh Your Way Through This Homebuilder's Wacky Story!

"You Want to Build and Fly a WHAT?"

by Dick Starks

This is the boisterous, very funny, wildly exaggerated true story of Dick Starks, a math teacher who goes through the agonies and delights of learning to fly, buys a down-at-the-tires Cessna, then goes on to build a replica of a WWI Nieuport fighter plane.

Dick becomes part of the Dawn Patrol, a group of airborne lunatics who fly out of a tiny strip and are constantly challenging one another to strange types of aerial combat.

His book is about the fun of flying and the joy of sharing that fun with family and friends.

> *"Dick Starks' tribulations and loss of innocence are your gain. His mixture of humor, philosophy, and technical stuff offers a unique insight into the slightly warped mind of a dedicated aircraft homebuilder."*
>
> – Dave Martin, editor of KITPLANES

•

> *"This boisterously funny, though somewhat exaggerated book about the adventures and mis-adventures of learning to fly and then building your own airplane will literally have you rolling with laughter. Yet, despite his zany humor, Starks has captured the real joy and cameraderie that somehow brings airplane folks together and makes those friendships so special."*
>
> – *Mary Jones, editor of* EAA Experimenter

256 pages, with hilarious illustrations by Bob Stevens

Only $12.95 plus $2 shipping. California residents add 94¢ tax

30-day money-back guarantee

VISA/MC: 1-800-648-6601

Or send check or money order to:

Butterfield Press

990 Winery Canyon Rd

Templeton, CA 93465